YOU NEVER SEE A HEARSE PULLING A TRAILER

MAYBE IT'S TIME
TO SPEND MORE
AND WORRY LESS.

D1056535

YOU NEVER SEE A HEARSE PULLING A TRAILER

Maybe It's Time
to Spend More
and Worry Less.

DAVID KENNON

You Never See a Hearse Pulling a Trailer: Maybe it's Time to Spend More and Worry Less

By David Kennon.

Investment advisory services provided through Kennon Financial, a registered investment advisor.

ISBN: 978-0-578-95034-1

Printed in the United States of America
by Serbin Print Marketing & Publishing, Sarasota, Florida

CONTENTS

Introduction

A re you afraid of running out of money in retirement? Don't feel bad, everyone does.

Why does this retirement planning stuff feel so complicated? (And why does spending your savings so terrifying?)

Over the past twenty years, I noticed that Baby Boomers were facing a real challenge when it came to retirement. They had been taught by their Depression-era parents to save-save-save. They had lived through stock market crashes and economic downturns. Worst of all, they had been fed a near-constant stream of doom-and-gloom from the financial media.

How can they possibly contemplate spending money in retirement? If they don't save every penny and watch every dollar, they may end up living in the Walmart parking lot eating Dinty Moore beef stew out of the can. Right?

Wrong.

Prepare yourself to be liberated by information that will show you to prepare for retirement, and how to make your retirement years as awesome as possible.

I've been a financial advisor for twenty years and I've noticed three things:

1. There is so much financial "noise" out there it is hard to know what to do or who to trust.
2. No one is explaining financial concepts in a way that you can understand. If you don't understand how retirement planning works, you can't help but worry.
3. Most of you want to enjoy your money you saved for retirement! You don't want to live in fear your whole life and end up with a bunch of money left over. I can't tell you how many times clients have jokingly told me, "I want the last check to the undertaker to bounce!"

The book in your hands is filled with short, financial articles that will tell you what you need to know in plain English you can understand. Be careful. You don't want to live poor and die rich. Maybe it's time to spend more and worry less!

What's with the Family Updates, Dave?

This is a journey we are making together, so why not get to know each other a bit? At the end of each article, I always include a Family Update. I have four kids, now ages 8,10,12, and 14. There is a lot of adorable hijinks in my house, and my newsletter subscribers told me they loved getting to know my family. I hope you do, too.

Warmest Regards,

Family Update

My youngest son, Jesse, really likes to cuddle his Mommy. He'll jump into bed with her each morning and shift around to get cozy.

He will always ask "Mommy, are you comfortable?" And if she says, "Yes." Then he says, "Then it's a *real* cuddle."

Important Notes

1. Due to the original publishing dates, some of the family updates may seem to be out of order.

2. If you find this book useful, PLEASE share it with your spouse. It is vital that both of you share the same understanding of retirement planning.

To sign up for future newsletters
OR
To do your own plan online
(based on my beliefs)

Go to:
www.StopLivingScared.com
or call 941-556-6307

YOU NEVER SEE A HEARSE PULLING A TRAILER

Reality check time. When you die, you cannot take your possessions or money with you.

Everybody knows this to be true, but on the flip side of the coin, when you retire and no longer have an income, it can feel like you need to hang onto every dollar, just in case. It can be a very stressful and scary transition. It is hard to spend your money once you are retired.

Most people are worried; you are not the only one.

What if I run out of money? What if I become a burden to my kids? What if I end up bagging groceries at Publix in my nineties?

These are all important questions, that I covered, in-depth in my book *The Retirement Revolution: Spend More, Worry Less.* What follows here is a summary of the book using short, easy-to-read chapters.

I bet there is something deep inside of you saying, "I've worked hard and saved my money all these years. When do I get to enjoy it?! Sure, it would be nice to leave a little to the kids. But this is MY money."

Do you feel like you can't have it both ways? Enjoy your retirement with your savings AND leave a little something for your kids? Do you worry that you'll run out of money? Hold onto your hats. The government statistics on retiree finances are shocking.

On average, retirees are dying with 60 percent more money than they had on the day they retired.[1]

Eighty percent of retirees are spending less money than what comes in each month.

So, what does all this mean?

If you don't start thinking about what your money is for, you could very well end up like 80 percent of the country who *underlives* and *oversaves*.

The alternative I am suggesting is not especially radical.

At its core, it contains a very reasonable and logical idea. Once you retire, you need to start spending some of your retirement savings *immediately*.

How much should you start spending? We will cover that in future lessons. But generally speaking: Once you retire it is okay to start spending the money that your money is making. If your CD is paying one percent, spend the one percent. If your portfolio of stocks and bonds are returning an average of five percent, spend the five percent.

Does that make sense? Spend the money the money is making. Whenever I sit down with retirees in their eighties and nineties, do you know what most of them say to me, "Why did I wait so long to spend my savings? I have more than ever. Dave, why didn't we have this conversation with you twenty years ago?!"

Regret. Needless worry. Oversaving. Underliving.

But this is not your destiny. You are going to take time to learn the facts. You are going to open yourself up to the idea that maybe there is a better way to handle retirement planning. You are going to find the perfect balance between spending and saving. You might end up living a much richer retirement than you realized.

Family Update

My oldest son Chris is growing like a weed. He's 12 years old and eats enough for five people. If we make a pizza, he can eat most of it by himself. If we get a sub, he finishes his and complains he is still hungry.

I came downstairs the other day and he was making an entire package of bacon for a snack. Probably fifteen pieces. Nothing else. All for himself.

Don't get too close or he will growl at you.

---

1. https://www.financialplanningassociation.org/

Don't Turn Into Your Parents

A re you worried you are going to run out of money during retirement? Do you feel an underlying sense of dread and unease whenever the subject of retirement planning comes up? You're not alone.

I get pretty passionate when discussing this, because I've seen the same weary, anxious look on the faces of far too many good, hard-working people like you. Why is this whole retirement thing so darn scary? You shouldn't have to live like this!

Retiring Baby Boomers are in the eye of the storm. Several different "fear factors" are converging together, all of them working to ensure you are as stressed as possible about your finances once you retire.

#1 Your parents were alive for the Great Depression. You are a product of your upbringing. You were told to "work hard and save, but never spend a dollar." If you do spend any money the sky will fall and you will end up living in a van down by the river.

#2 Pensions are a thing of the past. The golden age of defined benefit pension plans is long gone. No longer are people retiring to the security of a guaranteed pension. Now, it is up to you to plan for your old age.

#3 The financial media is hysterically negative. This irresponsible fear-mongering affects everyone. It is hard to stay calm when a guy, in a suit, on a major TV network, is saying things like, "The worst crash of our generation is coming." [2]

Without the benefit of my professional expertise, I'd be scared too!

#4 Your "safe" savings choices aren't working anymore. Interest rates are at historic lows. In the early 2000s you could have found a 5-year CD paying five percent without too much trouble.

But now, we are going on 15 years where CDs, money markets, and other "guaranteed" financial vehicles have been paying less than one percent. In many cases much less than one percent. Right now, nationally, the average interest rate on a savings account is .08 percent.

What does all this mean? Retirees, for the first time, are almost being forced to employ stocks and bonds in their retirement portfolio. What other choice do you have? Most people understand that getting .01 percent of their retirement savings is not the answer.

If you were living in 1981 right now you could walk into your friendly neighborhood bank and put your money into a three-month CD and get around 16 percent interest. Whoa! Who would even consider putting their money in the stock market if you could get 16 percent guaranteed at the bank?

Sadly, we are not living in 1981. But I have amazing news! You do not need to be scared of stocks and bonds. In fact, this unique interest rate environment might "force" you into utilizing the most powerful financial vehicle ever conceived by human kind. We will talk more about investing later in the book.

So I want you to be encouraged. The four "fear factors" working against you do not have to sabotage your retirement. With a little bit of education and planning you are going to thrive!

Family Update

Yesterday, my 6, 8, and 10-year-old boys were out dancing and playing in the rain in their underwear. I don't care who you are: that's cute. Yes, like any siblings, there are times they argue or even wrestle, but they share a bond that I believe they'll carry into adulthood. It sometimes makes me wish I had brothers growing up.

2. Business Insider, June 9, 2017. "JIM ROGERS: The worst crash in our lifetime is coming" https://www.businessinsider.com/jim-rogers-worst-crash-lifetime-coming-2017-6

Stick to the Facts

Too many people are waiting too long to start spending their savings once they retire.

That's not just my opinion. In fact, I'm going to try to convince you of the veracity of this statement with cold, hard data. Once I've presented my case, I hope many of you reading will come to the same conclusion I did long ago: The Retirement Revolution—a confidence-based approach to retirement planning and living—is a necessary wake-up call for Baby Boomers across America.

Here we go ….

Fact #1   The top 60 percent of Americans are not spending near enough money to put themselves in danger of running out in retirement.[3]

This data turns conventional wisdom on its head. Why is the conventional wisdom still … conventional? Because sensationalism and doomsday forecasting sell papers and makes ratings.

Fact #2   Over 75 percent of those over the age of 44 fear outliving their money more than death.[4]

It is nearly impossible to make measured, intelligent, and rational decisions about your retired financial future when it is basically scaring you to death.[4]

Fact #3 Two large national studies showed that, over the first 18 years of retirement, about one-third of seniors increased their assets.[5]

Do you know how many Baby Boomers live in this country? 76 million. Is it possible that one-third of them (25 million) will die with more money than they ever had before in their lives? Why? Because they've been scared out of spending any of it.

Fact #4 A person with less than $500,000 in savings, on average, spends just about a quarter of it during the first 20 years of retirement.[6]

Those of you with modest savings are not going to end up broke in 20 years if you have a sound financial budget and plan for retirement.

Remember, if you don't understand the plan your advisor gives you, it isn't really a plan.

Fact #5 According to the Center for Retirement Research, 48 percent of retirees are able to maintain their standard of living.[7]

Do you mean to tell me that almost half of the country will be able to spend the same amount of money retired as when they were working? Isn't that the ultimate goal in retirement planning? Half of the country will literally see no lifestyle change. Awesome!

Fact #6 According to the Employee Retirement Benefits Institute, 75 percent of retirees only take the federally mandated minimum withdrawal (RMD) from their IRAs (starting at age 72).

People are holding on to that retirement account absolutely as long as possible. Don't do that. Don't let the government determine when you can spend your savings.[8]

Fact #7 After Medicare premiums, the median lifetime cost for health care for a retiree from age 70 to death (95 or later) is slightly above $27,000, according to a new study by the Employee Benefit Research Institute. This is far less than conventional wisdom.

Anytime you hear that retirees need hundreds of thousands of dollars for medical expenses, take it with a grain of salt. That number is only true for a small part of the population.[9]

Fact #8 Sixty-four percent of retirees say that it is "very easy or somewhat easy" to pay their bills. The evening news doesn't give you that impression but it's true! [10]

Fact #9 In 2010, the U.S. census revealed that only 3.1 percent of retirees were in nursing homes. You probably know someone in a nursing home, and I want to be sensitive to that. But there is a small chance you will be living in a nursing home for a long time.[11]

Fact #10 The average spending for households headed by 55- to 64-year-olds was $65,000 in 2017, according to a Consumer Expenditure Survey. Spending dropped to $55,000 between ages 65 and 74, and after that it fell to $42,000. Spending dramatically decreases with age.[12]

So you're going to spend 35 percent less fifteen years into your retirement? Maybe you can spend more now!

Fact #11 Here are the median net worth's of Americans.[13]
Ages 45-54 $127,044
Ages 55-64 $191,836
Ages 65-74 $229,425
Ages 75 and older $271,162

Most people's net worth increases with age. This is the most powerful and game-changing statistic I can find. Why is nobody talking about this?!

Let's start talking about it. Tell your friends. Remind your spouse when they start to panic over a financial news story. These are the facts. Facts are empowering. They dispel fear and strengthen confidence.

Let's stick to the facts.

Family Update

We just bought a book full of "Dad Jokes." I can't get enough of these things. It is adorable to see my 8-year-old read some of them, pause for a second with a puzzled look in his eye, and then see his face brighten and say, "Ohhhhhh, I get it..."

I'm reading a book about anti-gravity. It's impossible to put down!

What does a zombie vegetarian eat? "GRRRAAAAAIIIINNNNS!"

Spring is here! I got so excited I wet my plants!

Why couldn't the bike stand up by itself? It was two tired.

I used to have a job at a calendar factory but I got fired because I took a couple of days off.

_____

3. New Retirement, June 27, 2020. "Retirement is All About Spending, And Experts Say You Aren't Spending Enough."
4. Seeking Alpha, May 19, 2016. "Afraid Of Outliving Your Money In Retirement? You're Not Alone.
5. Forbes, April 18, 2018. "Many Americans Go Broke In Retirement, But Many Others Gain Wealth In Old Age
6. Reuters, May 10, 2018. "The Myth of Outliving Your Retirement Savings"
7. Center for Retirement Research at Boston College
8. https://www.thinkadvisor.com/2018/08/31/how-rmd-rules-influence-ira/
9. FinancialPlanning, July 6, 2018. "Are You Overestimating Clients' Health Care Costs?
10. Center for Retirement Research at Boston College
11. www.seniorliving.org/statistics-about-seniors/
12. New York Times, 11/29/18, The Myth of Steady Retirement Spending, and Why Reality May Cost Less
13. Nerdwallet. Average Net Worth by Age: How Does Yours Compare? October 5, 2020.

Why Your Checking Account can be Your Best Friend

When I take on new clients there are certain rules that I ask them to follow. One of the most important rules is: As soon as you retire, each month you take an income check from your retirement and investment accounts, whether you need it or not.

Here's a quick example:

Mr. and Mrs. Smith retire with $500,000 in savings. We determine that by utilizing a diversified portfolio of stocks and bonds (with at least half of the money in stocks), it would allow them to withdraw $25,000 a year from their savings. Looking over 200 years of economic history, this is a sustainable and reasonable withdrawal amount.

Now, do Mr. and Mrs. Smith dip into their account whenever they need some money, making sure they don't go over the $25,000? No.

Do Mr. and Mrs. Smith take all $25,000 at once at the beginning of the year? No.

There is definitely a psychology to retirement spending and I've learned, over the past 20 years, that neither of these approaches works particularly well.

If you only dip into your account when you "need to," most people find it to be a painful experience. Remember, you are children of Depression-era parents. To many of you, withdrawing money from your retirement savings can conjure up thoughts like, "I hope this isn't a mistake. I hope I don't run out of money. This feels so irresponsible. This money doesn't even really belong to me, it belongs to retirement."

What about taking the $25,000 all at once? While this is a better option than above, I've found that generally speaking, human beings live their financial lives on a monthly basis. Most, if not all of your bills are due monthly. You've been getting paid monthly or bi-weekly your entire life. It can be difficult to budget a $25,000 lump sum to last the entire year.

After years of in-the-trenches financial planning experience, I've determined the best strategy, by far, is to receive income checks on a monthly basis. In the example above, Mr. and Mrs. Smith take their $25,000 over 12 months (or $2083/mo).

This not only allows you to know exactly how much money you can spend in any given month, but it also takes away the pain of withdrawing money from your retirement savings "as needed." For whatever reason, when human beings see their checking account growing as the investment income checks roll in each month, they treat that money differently than if it was still in their retirement savings accounts.

Think about this for a second. If you had $500,000 in your retirement savings and that account grew to $525,000 during the year, you might say to yourself, "Oh, that's nice. At least the money is growing." And then you go about your day and probably don't think much about it.

But if that $25,000 ended up in your checking account, you might say, "Wow! This is awesome. Instead of me working, my money is working for me. It's like I'm getting a 'paycheck' for doing nothing! How am I going to spend my money to make my retirement more awesome?"

As you can see, these are radically different experiences of the same investment result.

And don't forget, the central tenet of the Retirement Revolution is you need to spend the money you receive. You are not going to end up like the majority of Americans who are dying with significantly more money than they've ever had before in their lives.

You are going to live an empowered and fulfilling retirement armed with the knowledge that you are spending exactly the right balance between too little and too much.

So if, as you are receiving your monthly investment income check, you find yourself saying, "I had better stick this money in the bank and save as much as I can. I sure don't want to outlive my money." Stop!

Spend. The. Money.

I'm not telling you to become materialistic. I'm not telling you to buy stuff you don't really want or need. I'm telling you to live your life with a sense of opportunity and openness to reinventing yourself during your retired years.

So get those checks rolling in, spend the money, and find comfort in the fact that you have a plan in place that has stood the test of time.

Family Update

In a family of six, with four kids going to school, germs invariably make it home. And once an illness takes hold, it sweeps through the house (sometimes more than once). When it's Mommy's turn to get sick, that's when the wheels really fall off.

We suddenly must subsist on pizza, grilled cheese, and scrambled eggs. Bathing becomes optional and the kids' bedtime schedule is altered, resulting in crabby kids, resulting in an exasperated Dad, resulting in Mommy needing to come to the rescue while sick. My wife is truly my angel. I literally don't know what I would do without her. For even a week.

To sign up for future newsletters
OR
To do your own plan online
(based on my beliefs)

Go to:
www.StopLivingScared.com
or call 941-556-6307

Bagging Groceries at Ninety: Part One

L et's walk through the thinking process of a newly minted retiree who is going at this all wrong. In the next article (stay tuned!) we'll look at someone attacking the retirement bogeyman with logic and planning.

How much does the following sound like you?

The following conversation took place between Mr. Jones, 65, and his brain (also 65) shortly before his retirement.

Hmmmmm ... my last day of work is next week. It looks like I will get my last paycheck on Friday.

Okay, with Jane's Social Security and my Social Security we should be bringing in about $3,000 a month. Is that enough? It doesn't sound like very much.

My property taxes are $2,000 a year, homeowner's insurance is $2,000, car insurance $1,000, and the electric bill is around $200 a month .... (John begins to add up all their household expenses.)

Wait a minute, it looks like we are spending about $4,500 a month now. Crud. How is this going to work? I have $400,000 in my IRA, but I can't touch that. I might run out of money!

I don't know how this is going to work.

Wait a minute, I have my IRA invested in the stock market. Is that still appropriate for a guy like me? What if the stock market crashes!

That guy on the radio keeps saying that we are "due" for a crash. I guess maybe I should put the money in a money market? But that only pays 1 percent.

Maybe I should get a part time job? I think Home Depot said they were hiring. They pay around $10 an hour. So if I need an extra $1,500 a month I would have to work 150 hours.

Wait a minute! 150 hours! That's a full-time job.

Okay, John, think. Think. I am 65 years old. I am probably going to live at least another 20 years. So, if I take the $400,000 in savings and divide that by 20 years, it comes out to $20,000 a year. That is a little more than $1,500 a month. That could work.

But wait, Jane's Mom is still alive at 95. What if I die at 85 and Jane lives another ten years? I can't leave Jane destitute. She has put up with me for forty years already.

So maybe I should divide my savings into 35 years just to be safe. That gives me about $11,000 a year. So, I guess if we cut out our yearly vacation, and stop going out to eat so much, we can get the budget down to $4,000 a month. We should be Okay then.
But wait! What if one of us gets sick?! What if we need a new roof, a new air conditioner, or some other unexpected expense? The roof is 20 years old.

This is getting serious. How is this going to work?! We need to have some money set aside.

I guess Jane and I could both go work part time. But our health won't let us do that indefinitely. Jane is NOT going to be happy if she needs to work a part-time job.

Wait a minute! I'm not even considering inflation. $4,000 a month may not be enough in ten or twenty years. What are we going to do then?!

I need a stiff drink. I feel my chest tightening. Maybe I should turn on the financial news channel to get some ideas.

Actually, Mr. Jones is in much better shape than he realizes.

Family Update

It getting warm enough for my kids to start using the pool more often.

My youngest, Jesse, hates taking showers. I do not understand this at all. Why would you want to go around all dirty and smelly?

So each day after school, Jesse has to take a shower before he can do anything else. Yesterday he went swimming as soon as he got home. When my wife told him to go take a shower, he said, "I already took a shower. I just took one in the pool!"

I guess he's going to go to school smelling like chlorine tomorrow.

BAGGING GROCERIES AT NINETY: PART TWO

L ast week we examined the thoughts of a soon-to-be retiree. I argued his thoughts were faulty; worrying and stressing about questions which have good answers. Below you will find the same internal dialogue, but this time I am going to show you a realistic and healthy way of thinking.

Hmmmmm … my last day of work is next week. It looks like I will get my last paycheck on Friday.

Okay, with Jane's Social Security and my Social Security we should be bringing in about $3,000 a month. I had better put a budget together to get a real handle on my cash flow needs for each month.

(John spends a couple of hours on a detailed and accurate budget.)

It looks like over the past year we spent $49,400. That comes out to $4,100 a month. I'll round it up to $4,500 a month to give myself some room.

If I need $4,500 a month, how is this going to work? Where is the other $1,500 a month coming from?

If I divide my $400,000 in savings by 20 years I can pay myself around $20,000 a year. That gives me about $1500/mo. That is cutting it close, and what if we live longer than that 20 years?

Wait a minute.

I know my retirement savings can be invested in such a way that my nest egg continues to work for me.

It doesn't make any sense to just look at the money and divide it by the number of years I expect to live. I'm leaving out the most important variable. My money will continue to grow once I am retired.

I know that while it is impossible to predict the financial markets in the short term, between now and the day I die, we have a very good idea of how a diversified portfolio will perform.

Okay. From the $400,000 I can start withdrawing $1,500 a month made up of the money that the money is making. By only taking the profits, it doesn't matter how long we live, because we will always have the money we started with. History shows that we will probably end up with more than what we started with, even with taking $1,500 per month from the account.

That puts us right at $4,500. I guess I can still go to work part-time at the golf course. That sounds like fun, and it would get me out of the house. That income can be our "vacation fund."

If we have some unexpected major expenses like a new roof or air conditioner, I can draw some of the retirement account down. We could even have the flexibility to spend a little bit of the principal if we really need it. We don't need to die with the original $400,000 anyway. I want the last check to the undertaker to bounce!

Sure, nothing is guaranteed in this life. I guess there is always a small chance that we will experience something as bad as the Great Depression in the next few years. But what a terrible way to view my life! I don't want to spend all my time worrying about something that has such a small chance of happening.

I guess I should also worry about inflation. But wait! Social Security increases lock-step with the rate of inflation. If inflation goes up 2 percent for the year, my Social Security check will increase by the same amount. Not to mention that I'm sure Jane and I will be spending a lot less money in our eighties than our sixties.

Hmmmm ... I hope one of us doesn't get Alzheimer's or something and require comprehensive 24/7 medical care. Maybe I will try to spend as little money as possible for the time being. I can act like I am broke with lots of money in the bank. That care would be really expensive, and I don't want to run out of money.

Wait a minute! I saw that there is only a 10 percent chance of needing round-the-clock care for five years or more in a nursing home. If one of us does get sick enough to require full-time care (heaven forbid) it will most likely be near the end of our lives. I refuse to live the rest of my life preparing for a 10 percent possibility. I am going to focus on the 90 percent probability that I will live a long and healthy retirement.

Whew. I feel better. I need to get back to figuring out what I want to do in my retirement. I'm going to take my money each month from my investment accounts, spend my Social Security, and trust the process. I'm going to turn off the financial news channel, stop my subscription to Money Magazine, and tune out the inflammatory fear-mongering around me.

It's time for Jane and I to enjoy the fruits of our labor. I refuse to live scared and die rich!

<End Transcript>

You see? It takes a little re-education, but very few retirees end up living in the Walmart parking lot. The retirees you see bagging groceries generally are not doing it to survive. They are just looking for something to do.

Family Update

Senay loves Hallmark Christmas movies. I watched about 15 minutes of one and said, "I'm sorry, this is way too boring."

She turned around and replied, "Daddy, do all movies have to have machine guns and car chases?!"

Don't Read This if you Already Understand it

This week, let's get back to the basics.

Question: What is a stock and why do you make money when you invest in one?

Let's say your friend, Suzy, owns a car wash. The business is pretty successful. The cost of running the car wash is $10,000 a year, and the business brings in $12,000 a year. Suzy gets to pocket the $2,000 profit.

Suzy also has a gambling problem. She believes she has a fool-proof way of betting on sports, but, as it turns out, she doesn't.

Suzy needs money, and fast. She approaches you and says, "I will sell you part of my business. For $5,000 I will sell you a 50% stake."

Another way of saying this is: "You will own 50% of the stock in my business."

The next year love bugs are much worse than usual. Desperate citizens flock to the car wash. At the end of the year, the business shows a profit of $4,000. As a 50% shareholder, you receive $2,000.

If you invest in Apple you may own .00001% of the shares. So, you are eligible for .00001% of the profit. It is the exact same concept.

The more Apple grows, the more you make.

That's it. That's a stock.

Question: What is a bond and how do you make money when you invest in one?

Bonds are actually much easier to understand. A bond is a loan. You know when you put your money into a savings account and receive .01% interest? What does the bank do with your money?

They loan it out at much higher rates and pocket the difference. Banks are unbelievably profitable. That's why there is a bank on every corner.

So if you own a bond, in a sense, you are the bank. Let's say Sarasota Memorial Hospital is constructing a new building and they need money. They could issue a bond that basically says: "If you give us $10,000, we will give you one bond on which we will pay you 3% interest. At the end of ten years we will repay the loan back to you. You will get your $10,000 back."

You see? You are the bank.

I often wonder why people put money into savings accounts. You can skip the bank and just invest directly where the bank invests their money. But that is a topic for a future article.

Bonds are more stable than stocks, but stocks, historically, have returned far more. Risk equals reward.

Let's take a look at economic history. I want to extinguish the idea that these vehicles can lose a bunch of money.

What we are about to look at is the 5-year *average* return for indexes.

Question: What is an index?

The S&P 500 index is a composite of the 500 biggest companies in the U.S. The Bond index is a composite of thousands of bonds (loans).

I'm trying to make the point that while, yes, there are bad years here and there, it doesn't really matter.

Get ready to have your mind blown. Let's start with bonds. The Bond Index has been tracked since 1975.

The Worst Five Year Period:

An *average* return was 2.1% between 2012-2017.

The Best Five Year Period:

An average of 18.42% from 1981-1986 (this was during a time of hyperinflation. Bond returns and interest rates are closely related).

Since interest rates are so low, it is reasonable to assume low returns going forward, but still far higher than a CD. Was there **ever** a five-year return that averaged a negative number? **No**. In fact, there has never been a **two-year** span where the average was negative for bonds.

Next up are U.S. stocks. The S&P Index has been tracked since 1945.

The Worst Five Year Period for U.S. stocks

The markets returned an average of -2.3% from 2000-2005. The markets returned -2.3% on average from 1969-1974. That's it. Seriously, those are the only two times.

I really want this to sink in.

In modern economic history, there are two instances where the five-year average was negative and even those are low single digits. Why are you worrying? Be confident that five years from now your account will be worth more than now.

Please stop looking at your account every day. It. Doesn't. Matter. I want you to help your friends too. Next time you see them tell them the fact that:

Over any ten-year period, in economic history, the stock market has gone up.

Family Update

My Aunt Ruthie turned ninety-five last week. My middle son, Alex, wanted to make her coconut cupcakes from scratch. For a ten-year-old he can make a seriously good cupcake.

Sadly, Ruthie lives in my hometown of Pittsburgh so we were only able to see her through FaceTime. We sang her happy birthday, blew out her candles, and ate her cupcakes on camera. She was delighted.

PIE CHARTS CAN BE YOUR BEST FRIEND

Sometimes I forget that many of you don't understand some of the basics when it comes to investing. It is very easy for me to lose track when, not only have I been managing money for twenty years, but my Dad has a long history of investing as well. Did you talk about investing in stocks and bonds with your parents? Probably not.

So let's break this down to the absolute simplest terms possible. As I said, I often assume my readers understand certain concepts. If you don't, everything else may be hard to understand.

When most people invest money, instead of buying a bunch of individual stocks, they put the money into mutual funds. Mutual funds consist of hundreds or thousands of holdings within one investment vehicle.

When somebody says "You should have a diversified portfolio," it simply means you need to spread the money around. Mutual funds are a great way to do this.

I generally recommend against single stocks as they can be quite volatile and unpredictable. History shows a very predictable pattern of the total stock market, but individual stocks can do anything.

And I don't care if a company has been around for a long time. That does not mean it will make money. For example, GE has been around forever. It is down 65% over the past couple of years. Heinz is down 60%. Remember Texaco? It was one of the biggest companies in the country at the time. It went to zero.

When you buy a mutual fund, the mutual fund has a ticker symbol. You need to know the ticker symbol to buy the mutual fund.

Let's say, you walk into Charles Schwab or Fidelity, and you ask them to purchase $100,000 of SPY. What are you actually investing in? SPY is a fund that consists of the 500 largest companies in the U.S. all in one neat package. It means you would put:

$5,800 into Apple

$5,490 into Microsoft

$4,170 into Amazon

$4,070 into Google

$2,260 into Facebook

$1,480 into Berkshire Hathaway

$1,320 into Tesla

$1,290 into NVIDIA Corporation

$1,290 into JP Morgan Chase

$1,210 into Johnson and Johnson

$1,100 into Visa

$1,050 into United Healthcare

$920 into Proctor and Gamble

$910 into Home Depot

This list goes on and on until it totals $100,000. You will own shares in 500 companies. The bigger the company, the bigger the allotment.

Besides big American companies, there are other places to invest your money such as:

Small-Sized Companies (they are called "Small Cap")

Medium-Sized Companies (Mid Cap)

International Companies (Companies from first world nations)

Emerging Market Companies (Companies from developing nations)

You can also invest money in bonds. If you remember from past articles, a bond is simply a loan. For example, you loan Walmart $10,000 to help them build a store. They pay you 3% interest for ten years and then pay the loan back to you.

Bonds often do well when stocks are doing poorly.

The types of bonds are:

U.S. Government Bonds (You are loaning money to the U.S. federal government)

Municipal Bonds (Loans to municipalities)

Corporate Bonds (Loans to companies)

International Bonds (Loans to companies and governments overseas)

So a "diversified and balanced portfolio of stocks and bonds" might look like:

30% Large Cap

10% Small Cap

10% Mid Cap

10% International

10% Emerging Markets

10% U.S. Government Bonds

10% Municipal Bonds

10% Corporate Bonds

This is an example portfolio. I am not giving you advice on how to invest your money.

In addition, different asset classes move in different directions at different times.

In 2007 Emerging Markets made 40% and Small Companies lost 2%. Even though they are both technically "stocks," it doesn't mean their returns will be similar.

In 2013 Small Companies made 39% and Emerging Markets lost 3%. If you look above, you may notice that the returns flip flopped this particular year.

In 2008 U.S Treasury Bonds made 5% and Large Companies lost 37%. Oftentimes when the stock market is going down, bonds are going up.

In 2014 Large Companies made 14% and International lost 5%. International markets and the U.S. markets do not always move in the same direction.

Last year in 2020 Small Cap was the best with a 20% gain and Bonds were the worst with a 6% gain.

Also note that you do not want to "chase returns."

For example:

In 2017 Emerging Markets made the most and in 2018 they lost the most.

In 2018 Small-Cap was one of the worst and in 2019 it was one of the best.

Don't move all your money into an asset class because it did well the year before.

Even though everyone has opinions on what kinds of asset classes are going to do well in any given year, they have no idea what they are talking about.

Family Update

My two oldest kids are at camp and the two youngest are with Grandpa and Yaya. This is the first time we have been without kids at home for years. I guess when you are a Mom, if a kid is at home, no matter the age, you still need to be vigilant.

I haven't seen her this relaxed in a long time.

We got a chance to have an actual date consisting of Selby Gardens and dinner.

My Grandfather's Last Bank Statement

My grandfather (Papa) was a dearly loved elementary school principal. He retired in the 1980s with a modest teacher's pension. Papa never made more than $40,000 a year during his working life.

Papa lived a full and satisfying retirement all the way up to 89 years old. He was a great man, and still terribly missed. I remember each night I stayed at my grandparents' house, we would have the same routine. Papa would cut up an apple after dinner, and then we would go on the back porch and look for shooting stars. He adored my grandmother (Nana) and had two daughters. His daughters absolutely adored him. He was a gentle, loving, caring man and he modeled to me the kind of grandfather I want to be one day. He was a school teacher for a small, rural, community.

After he passed, we were going through his legal documents and financial statements after the funeral. We were rather shocked to discover that this very simple, humble man had somehow died with $900,000 in the bank.

As we searched through bank statements we made a startling (and typical) discovery. Papa had never stopped saving. Every month of his life, up to and including the last month, Papa scrimped and saved. I imagine he was quite proud that he was able to continue saving once retired (even though Nana and he also had a fear in the back of their minds.)

When my mom and my aunt learned of the money they remarked, "Why would Dad save all of this money? He and Mom could have done a lot more with it themselves. Of course, we appreciate this inherited money, but we wish they had spent more of it on themselves."

Papa was a teenager during the Great Depression so his views on savings and money were deeply ingrained. After several failed attempts, I have discovered that it is almost impossible to convince someone who was alive during the Great Depression to spend any of their money.

YOUR retirement doesn't have to look like your parents! You are going to reinvent and reimagine what this new and exciting stage of your life looks like.

You can embrace and attitude of, "I am not going to live in my fears. I am going to put a sensible plan together, and then focus on what I should be focusing on—living my most awesome retirement possible."

Family Update

Jesse is really getting into soccer. I woke up at 6:00 in the morning today and he was doing push-ups in a tank top in the living room. He has written out a training routine, which he has on the refrigerator that includes, "running around the house 40 times," "doing 20 somersaults," and "jumping 100 times." That is a cute thing to wake up to, *and* a great way to stay in shape.

The Four Most
Dangerous Words

To quote Sir John Templeton, "The four most dangerous words in investing are: this time it's different."

I'll show you what I mean through a few colorful anecdotes.

Robert Pinochle
The year was 1930. Robert Pincohle had $10,000 invested in the stock market. (A lot of money in 1930.) Robert thought to himself, "We are in the middle of the worst economic downturn this country has ever seen." He was right about that, but what he did next was a mistake. He thought, "This time is different. The markets are dangerous." Robert took all of his money in cash and buried it in his backyard. Ten years later, in 1940, his $10,000, had he kept it in the stock market, would have been worth $11,925.

John Canterbury
The year was 1940. John Canterbury had $10,000 invested in the stock market. He thought to himself, "We are in the middle of another World War. Countries are collapsing! The economic predictions are dire. This time is different!" John took the money in cash and stored it under the bed in his wife's best Tupperware. Ten years later in 1950, his $10,000, had he kept it in the stock market, would have been worth $35,035.

Earl Pickett
The year was 1950. Earl Pickett had $10,000 invested in the stock market. He thought to himself, "The Communists have infiltrated

our government. I'm pretty sure my neighbor Bob is a Commie. A Communist takeover spells disaster for our country, and the market. This time is different." Earl took the money in cash and hid it in his collection of Elvis Presley nesting dolls. Ten years later in 1960, his $10,000, if he had kept it in the stock market, would have been worth $44,694.

Paul Kowalski
The year was 1960. Paul Kowalski had $10,000 invested in the stock market. He thought to himself, "The stock market has been going up for nearly 20 years. We are due for a crash. This time is different." Paul took the money in cash and hid it in a Beatles lunchbox. Guess what? Ten years later in 1970, his $10,000, had he kept it in the stock market, would have been worth $21,959.

David Malkin
The year was 1970. David Malkin had $10,000 invested in the stock market. He thought to himself, "This country is falling apart. Vietnam. Oil embargoes. Hippies. This time is different." David took the money in cash and buried it in his backyard, putting his Pet Rock on top to guard it. Ten years later in 1980, his $10,000 would have been worth $22,555 ... if he had kept it in the stock market. Bummer, man.

Tom Chadwick
The year was 1980. Tom Chadwick had $10,000 invested in the stock market. He thought to himself, "The Cold War menace is looming. Nuclear tensions are at an all-time high. Russian paratroopers could descend from the skies at any time. This time is different." Tom took the money in cash and buried it in his backyard. Ten years later in 1990, his $10,000, had he kept it in the stock market, would have been worth $36,813.

Wolfgang Applebottom
The year was 1990. Wolfgang Applebottom had $10,000 invested in the stock market. He thought to himself, "Saddam Hussein has us on the brink of war. Stocks are overvalued. We haven't had a significant recession since the early 70s. This time is different. The markets are dangerous." Wolfgang took the money in cash and stuffed it into his wife's collection of Beanie Babies. Ten years later in 2000, his $10,000, had he kept it in the stock market, would have been worth $49,907.

Bobby Bickleberry
The year was 2000. Bobby Bickleberry had $10,000 invested in the stock market. He thought to himself, "The tech bubble is bursting. I'm hearing rumors of a long-term recession. This time is different. The markets are dangerous." Bobby took the money in cash and stored it in a safety deposit box at the bank. Ten years later in 2010, his $10,000, if he had kept it in the stock market, would have been worth $11,500 (after two of the worst bear markets in U.S. economic history).

Derek Johansen
The year was 2010. Derek Johansen had $10,000 invested in the stock market. He thought to himself, "We just experienced a decade with two historically awful recessions. I am spooked. No more investing for me!" Derek took the money in cash and locked it in a fire-proof safe, which he kept in his closet. Ten years later in 2020, his $10,000, if he had kept it in the stock market, would have been worth $34,715.

Maybe this time isn't different. Maybe it's time to embrace a financial vehicle that has an almost uninterrupted string of success for decades.

Family Update

We bought a waffle maker. It is a huge hit. My youngest, Jesse commented, "There is no such thing as too much waffle."

How to Only Work Three Hours a Day

It's 2020. A year for the history books. I figured we all needed some good news to fight the unrelenting negativity of the media. The following good news contains an important financial lesson. The human capacity to grow, change, and innovate is absolutely incredible. If you're worried about the stock market stopping its 200-year positive run, try this on for size:

In 1981, 42 percent of human beings lived in poverty. By 2018, that number had dropped to 8.6 percent.

The incidence of armed conflict has decreased substantially in the past few decades.

The chance of a person dying from a natural catastrophe (earthquake, flood, drought, storm, wildfire, or landslide) has declined 99 percent since the 1920s and '30s.

Ninety-percent of the world's population was illiterate in 1820. Today the world literacy rate is over 90 percent.

In 1870, the average time globally that a human being in the world spent in school was six months. That number is now eight and a half years.

The IQs of people across the world are growing at an incredible pace. IQ over the past hundred years has increased 30 points. How is that possible? No one knows for sure, but it probably has something to do with better nutrition, mentally challenging media, more schooling, and a reduction in childhood diseases.

Mothers died one-percent of the time during childbirth in the 18th century. Now it is 500 times less.

Smallpox, in the 20th century, accounted for between 300 and 500 million deaths. That is almost unimaginable. Prior to 1980, 30 percent of people who became infected died. Now the disease has been completely eradicated by vaccines.

Since 1990, the number of people dying from cancer has dropped by 17 percent due to advances in medical treatments.

Military spending is going down. In the past fifty years, 6 percent of the world's GDP (gross domestic product) was spent on the military. That number is now 2.2 percent.

In the past thirty years, homicide rates have been reduced by 17 percent.

For thousands of years the Earth was inhabited by hunter-gatherer societies. They worked between three and eight hours a day. Once they found their food, they stopped. Once we became more of an agrarian society, the average person worked between eight and twelve hours a day (depending on the time of year), six days a week. By 1830, the country was industrialized and the average American urban worker worked ten to twelve hours a day, six days a week. Today we stand at eight hours a day, five days a week. Even that has been reduced by 20 percent since 1950.

The number of countries with legalized slavery has dropped from sixty in the year 1800 to zero today.

One hundred years ago almost no land on Earth was deemed as "protected and regulated." Yosemite Park was one of the few. Today fifteen percent of the Earth is protected under these laws, which is twice the size of the United States.

Since 1910 economists have warned that the Earth is running out of oil. However, the world has pumped nearly one trillion barrels of oil since 1980. Oil reserves now stand at 1.7 trillion barrels. At the current rate of consumption, oil will run out in fifty years. Alternative energy is predicted to overcome the use of fossil fuels in the next 20 to 30 years. We may be left with a significant surplus of oil before it runs out; it appears energy may soon be renewable and infinite.

In the past fifty years, the prevalence of malnourishment in the world has dropped from 37 percent to 10 percent.

In the past thirty years, world access to electricity rose from 71 percent to 87 percent.

In the past thirty years, access to clean water in the world rose from 76 percent to 91 percent.

Seventy-three percent of Sub-Saharan Africa owns a smartphone. A Nigerian coal miner can send money to his mother in Lagos. A fisherman in the Congo can warn his friends about bad weather.

In the U.S., emissions of carbon monoxide fell 73 percent in the past thirty years.

Wow, that was a lot to take in. No matter what doom and gloom the media likes to heap upon you, never forget that we live in the wealthiest and safest world in human history.

All citations from *Ten Global Trends Every Smart Person Should Know by Ronald Bailey and Marian Tupy.*

Family Update

Summer is in full swing at the Kennon household. My oldest son Chris, who is 10, has been attending basketball camp. He seems to have some natural talent, which is amazing because he got zero genetic help from me. He insisted we get a hoop for the driveway and Dad played him one-on-one last night. Dad does not move like he did 15 years ago. Dad is sore.

To sign up for future newsletters
OR
To do your own plan online
(based on my beliefs)

Go to:
www.StopLivingScared.com
or call 941-556-6307

Ten Biggest Retirement Planning Misconceptions

After 15 years of "in-the-trenches" planning experience, I can tell you that I consistently see the same misconceptions come up time and time again among the Baby Boomer generation. Do not trivialize these misconceptions. It only takes one or two to really mess up your retired years.

For example, a very nice woman, who was about to retire, once told me that she didn't plan on ever spending any of her savings and investments. When I inquired as to why, she said, "You never know, I worry about medical costs. There is a history of cancer in my family."

I replied, "If you are enrolled in Medicare and if you have a Medicare supplement, the most you can be 'out-of-pocket' is less than $10,000 each year. If you get cancer and have a $400,000 medical bill, you are only responsible for less than $10,000 of it."

Without that tiny tidbit of information, this woman would have made every financial decision for the rest of her life based on a faulty understanding of the facts. She would have lived small, worried about money, and feared the future- for no reason.

So let's make sure you live the life you deserve.

Misconception #1: I need to have $1,00,000 to retire.

There is no standard amount of money that you need to possess in order to retire. It all depends on your savings, your monthly budget, and your expectations. Someone with $200,000 in savings and a monthly budget of $3,000 is probably going to be just fine. Someone with $2,000,000 in savings and a monthly budget need of $20,000 is probably in trouble.

Misconception #2:   The stock market is unpredictable and dangerous.

If you still believe this fallacy, please go to www.KennonFinancial. com and read my past commentaries (or keep reading this book). The stock market has a remarkably consistent, and successful, track record.

Misconception #3: Once I retire, I am too old to invest.

The life expectancy of a healthy 65 year-old is around 90 years old. Without utilizing growth investments, such as stocks, you are missing out on a powerful tool. I'm not promoting that you put all of your money in the stock market, but a diversified portfolio of stocks and bonds is usually appropriate throughout your entire lifetime.

Misconception #4: Super-smart people make more money investing than "normal" people.

There is zero academic evidence that anyone can outperform the markets. In other words, no one has a magical secret that will make your money grow faster than everyone else.

Misconception #5: If the stock market crashes, it could take decades for my savings to recover.

Not true. It took less than four years to recover losses from the 2008 crash. 2001 crash? Four year recovery. 1987? Just one year. 1973-74? Four years. 1939-40 took three years. Even the Great Depression losses were recovered in 4-½ years. Just get that belief out of your mind. Markets recover faster than you think.

Misconception #6: Social Security is going to go bankrupt.

I stay very close to developments within the Social Security Administration. I can find no evidence that your benefits are going to get cut. Luckily for you, it is easier for politicians to keep kicking that can down the road. Cutting benefits is absolute political suicide. My kids need to worry. You do not.

Misconception #7: I need to have my house paid off before I retire.

While it might feel nice to be debt-free, it is not a prerequisite for retiring. As long as your retirement budget can handle the payment, many people retire with a mortgage.

Misconception #8: I need to be super-vigilant on financial news and adjust my investments constantly.

No, you don't. Believe it or not, people back in the 70s and 80s only got market news once a week (gasp).

Misconception #9: I shouldn't spend any retirement savings unless I have to.

If you still believe this widely-held misconception please read my past commentaries or listen to my previous radio show episodes. It is absolutely responsible and prudent to withdraw a reasonable amount of money from your retirement accounts each month.

Misconception #10: Some people lose ALL their money in the stock market.

While this may be possible if you put all of your money into a single stock or a single bond, a diversified portfolio of stocks and bonds has never gone to zero. In fact, in the past fifty years, the WORST year for an investor with a 50/50 stock/bond portfolio was 1974. You would have lost about 12 percent overall for the year. By the way, the same portfolio would have been up 20 percent the following year.

Family Update

My youngest, Jesse, is experiencing some problems at school. Whenever his kindergarten class has recess, the girls run around the playground trying to kiss him. It's getting so bad that one girl got a red mark because she kissed him five times in one day. Red marks are serious business. Does Jesse like all the attention? No. Kissing is gross.

I don't remember ever being chased by girls at any point in my childhood or adult life.

The Investment Chart that Changed the World

Get ready. This article is the basis for my entire investing strategy. When I discovered the following facts, it permanently changed my financial planning philosophy.

If you are a numbers person, you are going to love this.

Whenever someone says to me, "The stock market is crazy. It goes up and down. I have no idea if I'm going to be Okay."

I think to myself, "But it doesn't matter. It just doesn't matter. Investing in a diversified portfolio has never NOT worked."

So what exactly do I mean by a diversified portfolio always works?

This week I am going to give you a glimpse into the appendix from my first book: The Retirement Revolution: Spend More, Worry Less.

I can't emphasize this enough. The historical data below simply shows you what would have happened if you had retired in any given year (starting in 1931). Each "retirement" is assumed to last 20 years.

The first row reveals what would have happened if someone retired in 1931 with $100,000. The money is invested in the 500 largest companies in the U.S. (otherwise known as the S&P 500 Index).

Starting with $100,000, the chart shows what would have happened if you started withdrawing $5,000 (or 5 percent) per year beginning the very first year of retirement. In each example, over 20 years, you would have withdrawn a total of $100,000 ($5,000 per year for 20 years).

I know this is technical, hang in there.

So, if you retired in 1941, over the next 20 years your money would have grown to $1,194,776 even though you withdrew 5 percent of the original investment each year.

So why is this so vitally important to understand?

One-hundred percent of the scenarios result in you ending up with more money than you started with. Eighty-six times in a row.

It is statistically correct to say, "Over the past 86 years, if you started with $100,000 and withdrew $5,000 per year for 20 years, you would have ended up with more than the original investment. Every. Time."

Hopefully, this blows your mind as much as it did mine! It doesn't matter what the stock market is doing.

Here is the chart. For example, pick your birth year, or your kid's birth year. Imagine if you retired that year and look at the value 20 years later, even though you had been withdrawing 5 percent.

This table makes the following assumptions:

1. You start with $100,000 invested in the 500 biggest companies in the U.S. (The S&P 500)
2. You withdraw $5,000 per year for twenty years. (Five percent of the original $100,000)
3. Each example below shows someone receiving $5,000 a year for 20 years. This equals a total of $100,000 received during those 20 years. ($5,000/year x 20 = $100,000)

Data and Calculations provided by Thomson-Reuters

Retired Years	Ending Value (what's left over)	Average Rate of Return
1931-1951	$513,210	11.4%
1932-1952	$766,022	13.27%
1933-1953	$386,712	10.15%
1934-1954	$660,031	12.56%
1935-1955	$431,282	10.63%
1936-1956	$219,962	7.84%
1937-1957	$633,616	12.37%
1938-1958	$589,235	12.03%
1939-1959	$735,558	13.08%
1940-1960	$966,123	14.40%
1941-1961	$1,585,122	16.91%
1942-1962	$1,194,776	15.46%
1943-1963	$1,118,421	15.13%
1944-1964	$1,066,591	14.89%
1945-1965	$786,149	13.39%
1946-1966	$867,869	13.87%
1947-1967	$1,062,546	14.87%
1948-1968	$1,169,095	15.35%
1949-1969	$903,770	14.07%
1950-1970	$679,685	12.70%
1951-1971	$604,166	12.15%
1952-1972	$597,148	12.10%
1953-1973	$552,969	11.74%

1954-1974	$227,119	7.97%
1955-1975	$204,629	7.57%
1956-1976	$241,785	8.21%
1957-1977	$292,907	8.98
1958-1978	$174,859	6.99%
1959-1979	$176,891	7.03%
1960-1980	$252,335	8.38%
1961-1981	$155,386	6.57%
1962-1982	$251,568	8.37%
1963-1983	$217,461	7.80%
1964-1984	$175,399	7.00%
1965-1985	$187,660	7.25%
1966-1986	$321,308	9.36%
1967-1987	$223,717	7.91%
1968-1988	$220,163	7.85%
1969-1989	$410,199	10.32%
1970-1990	$398,713	10.28%
1971-1991	$428,851	10.60%
1972-1992	$340,207	9.60%
1973-1993	$583,058	11.98%
1974-1994	$1,055,377	14.84%
1975-1995	$958,459	14.36%
1976-1996	$891,251	14%
1977-1997	$1,447,113	16.44%
1978-1998	$1,818,318	17.64%
1979-1999	$1,840,805	17.70%
1980-2000	$1,180,094	15.40%
1981-2001	$1,202,665	15.50%
1982-2002	$763,294	13.25%
1983-2003	$777,933	13.34%
1984-2004	$845,961	13.75%
1985-2005	$634,571	12.38%
1986-2006	$603,834	12.15%
1987-2007	$624,349	12.30%
1988-2008	$332,734	9.51%
1989-2009	$288,562	8.92%
1990-2010	$373,397	10%
1991-2011	$264,524	8.57%
1992-2012	$290,416	8.95%
1993-2013	$350,521	9.73%
1994-2014	$417,526	10.48%
1995-2015	$265,008	8.58%
1996-2016	$214,993	7.76%
1997-2017	$145,177	6.33%

Family Update

Last week I mentioned that my kids got me a bunch of board games for my birthday. We are having a lot of fun, and now they are getting into card games. At this point we have to keep it pretty simple. My 7-year-old is not ready for bridge.

Here are the card games we are playing. Which do you remember?

WAR   CRAZY EIGHTS   GO FISH   SNAP   SPIT

DO YOU WANT TO BE
REMEMBERED AS GENEROUS?

H ow much money is going to pass to heirs in the next 30 years? According to Time magazine, the number could reach over $30 trillion. Yes, that is $30,000,000,000,000.[14]

Today I am going to offer an alternative to leaving money to your kids.

Whenever I create long-term spending plans for my clients, I often hear, "But Dave, I understand you want us to start spending some money as soon as we retire, but we don't need the money. We don't even know what to do with it. We've learned to live frugally over the past forty years. We really don't need anything else."

"It's awesome that you've built up those habits," I'll usually reply, "That is a big part of why you are in the position that you are in. But if you don't use your money, someone else will—maybe the government, maybe your heirs—but you need to seriously think about what this money is FOR."

No one will ever be as good a steward of your savings as you. Let me say that again for maximum impact: *No one will ever be as good a steward of your savings as you.*

You've worked for it, you've earned it, you appreciate it. You have a more intimate connection to your money than anyone else ever could.

You hear about it all the time. Kids inherit their parent's money and it causes discord. They waste it. They fight with their siblings. They don't treat it with the same care and respect as their parents did.

Athletes sign huge contracts, oftentimes straight out of school. They blow through the money because they weren't prepared for it.

Many lottery winners say that winning the jackpot was one of the worst things that has ever happened to them. They don't know how to steward the money because they didn't earn it.

Of course, you need to do the appropriate planning to ensure you don't outspend your savings, but once you make sure you are not mortgaging your future, you get to start determining how you want to spend the money—right now.

I want to be very clear. I am not asking you to become materialistic. I am merely suggesting that you start living your life with a renewed sense of opportunity.

Which brings me back to your kids. As opposed to leaving them a large lump sum of money at your death, I think there's a better way.

Give them a little bit each month now. Or, put another way, dole out their inheritance a little bit at a time for the next 20 or 30 years.

Of course, we don't want to enable our children; you will have to make that determination.

Members of the Retirement Revolution already know that they are going to spend 5 percent of their retirement savings each year, starting the first year of their retirement. Some of that money could go to your kids now.

The benefits are numerous.

Benefit #1:   Your kids are in their twenties, thirties, and forties which are the most complicated and difficult times in somebody's financial life. They are having children. They are buying homes. They are starting careers. This is when they need the money. By the time you're gone, your kids could be in their sixties and seventies.

Benefit #2:   You are able to see your kids actually use and appreciate the money. You get to attend your granddaughter's piano recital (you paid for the lessons). You get to see the relief on your son's face when he realizes they are able to replace the car that keeps breaking down.

Benefit #3:   You are able to see how your kids treat the money. Are they acting responsibly? Are they making good financial decisions? Better yet, you can mentor and guide them on how to better manage their assets. And if they blow your cash?

Well, it's certainly better you know now.

Benefit #4:   It is tax efficient. Taking out a little money from your retirement accounts each month stretches out the tax liability. It is much better to take a little bit of money out each month versus large lump sums here and there.

While heirs are able to utilize a "stretch IRA," which can spread out their tax liability over ten, I often see IRAs cashed out completely. A $500,000 IRA is cashed out by your heir could result in over $150,000 in taxation.

(Mega) Benefit #5:   You are teaching your kids an incredible lesson about generosity. Your kids get to see, first hand, that Mom and Dad are not materialistic, nor are Mom and Dad overly stingy. Mom and Dad place value on what really IS valuable. Relationships. Family. Love and kindness.

If your kids see your generosity, they will grow to be generous themselves. Your legacy will last for generations.

Family Update

Our cat Turbo, who has a weight problem. All the kids make fun of him, and I think it hurts his self-esteem. We tried diet food and he refused to eat it. We tried to feed him less of his normal food and all he did was cry and cry—to the point that we figured it was easier to let him stay fat than let him complain. We even put him on an exercise regime where he has to chase lizards at least thirty minutes a day.

14. Time, February 13, 2013. "Boomers Never Got Their $30 Trillion Inheritance–But Will Millennials?"

Five Financial Myths the Media Wants you to Believe

For those of you who know me, you realize by now that I am a passionate guy. (For those of you who don't know me, just trust me on this.) When I am happy, I am overjoyed. And when I am upset, I am a teakettle at full boil.

One thing that really gets my blood boiling is anything that derails my clients from living their best life. And oftentimes, my anger is directed toward the financial media.

Don't get me wrong, the financial media is not innately evil. But here is an ugly truth they don't want you to think about: they only exist to sell advertising. It takes a lot of content to fill all those hours on TV and radio programming, and much of the time the financial media is propagating ideas that are not only wrong, but harmful to your financial health.

In fact, I spend a lot of my time helping people tune out 95 percent of the noise out there that does nothing to help their financial futures

Here are 5 myths the financial media wants you to believe. And why you shouldn't.

Myth #1: If you don't pay attention to the markets, your investments will suffer.

Of course CNBC wants you to believe that following the markets on a minute-to-minute basis is important—how else can they keep you watching all day?

I think Warren Buffett put it best: "I would tell (people) don't watch the market closely... The money is made by investing and by owning good companies for long periods of time. If they buy good companies, and buy them over time, they're going to do fine...If they're trying to buy and sell stocks, and worry when they go down a little bit ... and think they should maybe sell them when they go up, they're not going to have very good results."

Myth #2: You need to listen to the "super-smart Wall Street guys" in order to be a successful investor.

Nope. Not remotely true.

In fact, the longer I manage money for clients, the less I listen to anyone's "opinion" on the markets. For example, in 2017 this was the title for one article on Money.com, "It's Going to Collapse: 5 Scary Stock Market Predictions From Smart Investors."

The markets are up 50 percent since then.

If you were one of the poor souls who read that article and sold your investments, you would have missed out on a big run in the markets.

Nobody knows when the stock market is going to go up or down. There has not been a single human being in history who has been able to consistently predict the ups and downs of the markets.

Every once in a while, one of these guys gets lucky and guesses right. They then proceed to promote that fact for the rest of their lives. If you are right once and wrong 100 times, why does the financial media keep interviewing you? (Spoiler alert: It's about filling air time.)

Myth #3: Market experts know why markets go up and down.

I hear it all the time … the market drops a few hundred points and the media has all kinds of rationales. "Bad unemployment numbers came in." "Chinese currency fluctuations are affecting exports." "Instability in the Middle East is unnerving investors."

I have a counter-cultural truth for you here. The vast majority of the time, nobody, not even after the fact, truly knows why the markets went up or down.

They can hypothesize as to some reasons why it might have fluctuated, but no one ever knows for sure. The reality is, most movements in the market come from irrational human fear and greed. And human behavior is notoriously hard to predict.

Myth #4: It is important to continually buy and sell stocks inside your portfolio to maximize returns.

Here they go, filling air time again.

If Jim Cramer were honest, he would say, "These stocks might go up or might go down. Nobody really knows. But what we do know is that a long-term, disciplined strategy has proven to be incredibly effective at building wealth."

Of course, if he actually admitted that, there would no longer be any reason for him to have a show. Bad for Cramer, bad for advertisers. Better for you.

By the way, according to a study1 at the Wharton School at the University of Pennsylvania, Jim Cramer does not beat the market with his predictions. You would have been better off putting all of your money in the S&P 500 and just letting the money sit. "Cramer Picks" under-performed the market as a whole. Not to mention the cost of trading and the impact of taxes can be substantial when you are constantly buying and selling stocks.

Myth #5: Financial advisors watch the financial media to get the information they need to help their clients.

No, we don't.

I can't speak for everyone in my field, but I can say that I have never met a fellow advisor who buys and sells stocks based on what some guy on Fox News Business says.

With the advent of the internet, a universe of information is readily available at the fingertips of anyone with a cell phone. Nobody is going to say something on TV that hasn't already been revealed and researched by thousands of investors on the internet.

This is a big reason why the concept of a "hot stock tip" seems so antiquated. There really is no such thing anymore. Now, if anything, my main job is to help my clients determine what they need to save and what they can spend. It's about planning, not frantic buying and selling.

The other part of my job is sifting through the deluge of information my clients (and all of you) are subjected to, and discern what is actually relevant. Ninety-five percent of the financial information you receive is just noise.

It's important to recognize what the financial media is: Entertainment. Nothing more and nothing less. Don't let them derail you from sound planning and long-term investing.

Family Update

The kids are at vacation Bible school this week. I think they are having a great time. They come back absolutely exhausted, but they still enjoy showing off the cheers and songs they've learned while we eat dinner.

At camp there is a competition to see which group can yell the cheers the loudest. My kids are definitely trying their best. Alex almost totally lost his voice and the other kids all sound a little hoarse.

Apparently, they also have the best snow cones in the world.

Being Rich is Overrated

Over the past twenty years, I've met a lot of different people who possess different amounts of savings. I've met many people with nothing. I've met millionaires. I've met lucky dogs who have tens of millions of dollars. I have never met a billionaire.

It sure would be nice to be rich, wouldn't it?

Maybe not.

I have noticed a striking phenomenon throughout the years. The amount of money you possess has a diminishing return on your happiness and enjoyment of life.

What does that mean? Let me show you through a few illustrative anecdotes.

Meet George.
George is close to broke. He owns a small home without a mortgage, but he and his wife must survive solely on Social Security benefits of $2,700 per month. That's pretty tight.

I've done hundreds of budgets with clients and I've found that — in Sarasota, one of the leading retirement spots in the country — if you have no mortgage, you can get by pretty well on $4,000-$5,000 a month.
But, at $2,700 a month, George and his wife really need to be careful. They can probably only own one car. Probably can't go out to eat much, and need to clip every coupon. They will get by, but

a broken air conditioner can put incredible stress on their lives. In fact, I am willing to bet George and his wife live with a lot of daily stress over finances.

I don't want to live like George.

Meet Nancy.
In addition to her Social Security, Nancy and her husband have cobbled together about $400,000 in savings. They own their home and their Social Security totals $3,200.

Nancy invested her $400,000 in a balanced and diversified portfolio of stocks and bonds, with more than half the money in stocks. It is reasonable for her to withdraw $1,600 a month from the account without putting herself in danger of running out of money.

This now equals $4,800 a month, which is much more doable. They go out to eat a few times a month, at moderately-priced restaurants. They made a game of finding the best dinner specials in town. She and her husband play golf on the municipal courses, which keeps them both social, active and healthy.

They even take a small but nice vacation once a year. Nothing fancy, but great memories nonetheless. While this is not a lavish lifestyle, I've found the Nancys of the world can be perfectly content with her $5,000 a month. Of course, there are things she wishes she could do, but the European river cruise and new kitchen just aren't in the cards. It doesn't bother Nancy all that much. She has a roof over her head and can buy what she needs.

Meet Bob.

Bob was an executive at a small company in Tampa. His salary was in the six figures, and, together with his wife, they were able to save $1.2 million dollars. "I can't believe we're millionaires," Bob would often think.

With their house paid off, Bob and his wife, between Social Security and investment dividends, brought in $9,000 per month. After taxes that left $8,000 a month in cash, deposited straight into their bank account.

Now, this is some pretty serious money. Their budget was only $5,000 per month, which gave the couple $36,000 a year of "play money."

Bob and his wife travel. Alaska, Europe, and New Zealand. They replace the floors and added a patio on the back deck. Bob plays golf at some of the nicer public courses. They go out to eat basically whenever they want. Every once in a while, they really splurge on a good steakhouse dinner.

While Bob and his wife enjoy the money, they find that, after a few years, spending $36,000 of play money is unnecessary. They find a new source of joy in giving generously to their church and spoiling their grandchildren.

Bob and his wife ended up well-traveled with an upgraded home, living a quiet life they enjoyed.

Lastly, meet Charlene.

Charlene was rich. Between her Social Security and her investments, she realized about $20,000 a month in retirement income. This gave her nearly $100,000 of play money per year, while living a very nice lifestyle.

Charlene's husband is a member of an exclusive country club and plays golf at their world-famous course now and then. Even though it is only the two of them, they live in a brand-new, exquisite 4,000 sq/ft house, which they can easily afford.

They travel whenever and wherever they choose. African safaris, cruises to far off exotic lands — always in the upgraded suite of course — and other adventures. They eat at the finest restaurants, own the finest clothes, and have the best of just about everything. Charlene and her husband quickly ran out of ideas on how to spend the money. They had everything they wanted.

What is the point, Dave?

George (the broke one) desperately needed more money. His current income put him under incredible stress. He had to watch every penny.

Nancy is your standard professional woman. She saved some money which allowed her to do some of what they wanted, but the cheap version.

Bob, with his one million dollars, had a lot of opportunities. He and his wife traveled, and they found other, fulfilling ways to spend their money.

Charlene could do whatever she wanted. She and her husband belong to a fancy country club, eat wherever they want, and take exotic, exclusive vacations all over the world.

The difference from George to Nancy is significant. But, the difference between Nancy and Bob is actually pretty small. They both play golf. Maybe the greens were not quite as nice at Nancy's municipal course, but the game is just as fun.

The difference between Bob and Charlene is smaller than you would think. I can tell you, from personal experience, a five-star French restaurant's food doesn't taste all that much better than the nice Mom and Pop place down the street. Nancy and Bob were basically eating at the same places. Both got to travel.

Now, here's an important point: Nancy, Bob, and Charlene all had the same amount of fun on their trips. Maybe Bob and Charlene got to take more trips to more exotic locations. But is that really that big of a deal?

Charlene's Mercedes gave her no more joy than Nancy's used 2014 Honda CRV.

Nancy, Bob, and Charlene all ended up eating at essentially the same restaurants.

They all got to enjoy being terrible golfers.

I don't want to be George. You don't want to be George, either. (Sorry, George!)

Not having enough in retirement is a very tough situation. But, as for Nancy, Bob, and Charlene — they all lived relatively similar retirements.

Being "rich" does not give you all that better of a life compared to the "kinda-rich" compared to the "working/middle class." Sure, the levels of fanciness are different, but does it really matter that much if your hotel room has newer furniture than the other?

Don't have a false impression that more money means a totally different retirement lifestyle. It doesn't. I've done this for 20 years. It doesn't.

As long as you have enough to not worry about paying the bills, like George.

We have been put on this Earth for relationships. The relationships you have in your lives are far more important than your monthly income. The cliché is true — I've met very wealthy, lonely people, and I've met people without a penny to their name with lives full of love.

Family Update

My kids were able to go trick-or-treating on the golf cart. They were absolutely thrilled at how many generous neighbors gave full size candy bars!

My kids wanted to make sure they got a lot of Daddy's favorites to share. Namely Milky Way and Nestle Crunch.

Two of the three boys wore out pretty quickly, but my middle son, Alex, wanted to keep going.

He and his sister Senay can butt heads sometimes, and she was having a sleepover with a couple of her best friends. When they took over the golf cart and started out into the night, she let her brother tag along.

What a sweetheart.

THE TIME MACHINE GAME

L et's all get into my time machine and go back to 1995.

Zzzzzrrrrrr. Pfft. Bop. (Those are time machine noises.)

We made it. Here we are in 1995. You are retiring today and you have $100,000 to invest.

With that $100,000, you place 30 percent in bonds and 70 percent in stocks (the Barclay's Aggregate Bond Index, and the S&P 500 index).

This is a somewhat generic portfolio mix.

You then decide to start taking out $5,000 a year from your $100,000 investment.

Remember, it is 1995 and you have just retired. You decide to go live on a secluded island in the Caribbean. The island you choose has no internet (it's barely even a thing in 1995), TV, radio, or newspapers. In fact, you have absolutely no idea what is happening in the outside world.

For 25 years you stay there, enjoying your tropical "off-the-grid" lifestyle. The only connection you have to the outside world is that each year $5,000 shows up in your Bahamian bank account from your initial $100,000 investment.

In July of 2020, you return to the United States for the first time in 25 years. I am using this specific time period on purpose. In hindsight, those were a rough 25 years in the economy. Remember, in this time-traveling example, you have no idea what is happening to the world economy. You don't know that the market crashed in 2001 due to an internet bubble. You don't know that 2008 experienced one of the worst economic disasters in history.

You have never once looked at a financial statement. All you know is that over the past 25 years you have received $5,000 each year for a total of $125,000 from your investments.

You go online to check your investment account. You are more than a little nervous. Is there any money left? Your hand trembles as it clicks on the "login" button. What is the account balance remaining? Are you broke?! Should you have been keeping an eye on your portfolio, obsessively checking the stock ticker every hour over the past 25 years?

The remaining balance: $415,000

Started with $100,000. Took out $125,000. Now, you have $415,000.

You may be thinking, "Dave, are you actually telling me I don't have to be hyper-vigilant with my accounts? Are you saying that "staying on top" of my investments is unnecessary? Are you saying that I should put a good plan in place and then trust the process? Are you saying I don't need to worry at all?"

Yes, that is exactly what I'm saying. Plan. Invest. Live.

Family Update

It's prime campfire season here in Florida. Considering we only get a couple months of "cool" weather during the year, my kids and I have limited opportunities to build fires in the backyard. All three boys have learned how to build a proper campfire.

They have also mastered the art of roasting marshmallows. You need to be patient and create a nice brown, crunchy outside, while maintaining a soft, gooey inside. It is a skill handed down to me by my Mom and will now continue on through the next generation.

Let's be Chicken Little
for a Day

For about 50 percent of retiring Boomers, you retire you need to start spending a reasonable amount of savings each year as soon as you retire. My rule of thumbs is to "spend the money the money is making." If your CD is paying 2 percent, spend the 2 percent. If your stock and bond portfolio is returning an average of 5 percent, spend the 5 percent.

"But Dave," I keep hearing, "nobody can guarantee the future. While what you say is logical and sensible, you never know what might happen."

Okay, if that's the way we want to think, let's go down that road.

Story #1

Joan Smith retires and starts spending her money in a responsible and reasonable manner, making sure never to spend the principal, but enjoying the interest and dividends her investments paid out.

She uses the money on things she enjoys—things that are important to her. She spends more time with her kids and grandkids. She spoils herself at the spa from time to time. She goes out to dinner with friends. She confidently lives her retired years, knowing that she has a plan in place.

In fact, as she reaches her late seventies, she really starts to spend some money. "You can't take it with you", she always says. She buys a small condo for her sister who was recently widowed. She organizes and finances a large cruise/family reunion with her extended family.

Sure, she was spending the principal, but she figures, "I'm not going to live forever."

Then it happens. Early in her 90's the money starts running out. "I never thought I would live this long," she quips. She is reduced to living on her Social Security, small pension, and the small amount of money left over.

Is she thinking to herself, "What a horrible mistake!"

No! Joan had such a great retirement. She enjoyed her kids and grandkids. She deepened relationships with people she loved most. She helped people in need. Do you really think she would have looked upon her retirement spending as a mistake? Do you really think she would look back on her life with regret? Of course not! She's 92 years old. Her bucket list has been achieved. She might not live high on the hog anymore. *But she's 92 years old.*

Story #2

Jane Clark has found herself in financial trouble. After making a few poor decisions (including investing in a new apartment project in Puerto Rico), she found herself with very limited savings in her late sixties. Her daughter offers to let her mom move into their home.

"This is my worst nightmare," Jane thinks to herself. "I am a burden to my children. I can't believe this is actually happening to me."

But, as Jane settles into her new life living with her daughter, son-in-law, and three grandkids, she discovers something awesome.

Living with her daughter is a joy. Her grandkids desperately need more attention from their busy parents, and Jane is able to help out.

Her daughter feels blessed for helping out her Mom. Jane's grandkids will be forever changed by her presence in their life. "Life is funny," Jane chuckles to herself. "My worst fear ended up being one of the best things that ever happened to me."

Story #3

John White always worried that the economy was going to collapse. Once he retires, his worries get even more intense. "I'm not going to spend a nickel unless I have to. I am going to grow and defer this money as long as possible. Because you just never know...."

Well, in this example, John's fears came true. The economy faltered. In fact, the country started to experience such economic devastation that the landscape of the U.S. started to look more like the Great Depression than the 21st century.

Banks began to fail. People, desperate for their money, begin rioting and looting. The stock market drops 80 percent. A majority of Americans begin to default on their mortgages. Thirty-percent of the population is homeless. Marauding bandits fill the streets, making a simple trip to the store a potential exercise in hand-to-hand combat.

John sees his investments and cash evaporate. The nightmare he had always imagined had arrived.

So my question is: Did it matter that John deferred and grew his savings? No. No, it did not.

If this scenario were to actually happen, we are all in the same boat. In fact, if anything, John missed out on the only chance he had to enjoy the money. By the time economic Armageddon arrived, he lost everything anyway.

Story #4

Janice Smith always worried about needing nursing home care. She never spent a penny of her savings. Twenty years into her retirement, Janice developed dementia and ended up in a 24/7 nursing care facility.

The nursing home used up all of her money over the next few years. Janice, with the disease progressing, was completely unaware that her life savings were being drained. Looking back, maybe Janice should have used some of the money on things that were important to her while able.

Let's try to keep things in perspective. These fears you may have in the back of your mind, if they really were to play out, may not have the consequences you expected.

Family Update

My son, Chris, got glasses. He is pleased. He says they make him look smart. As a seventh grader, I am starting to notice that style and "being cool" is started to rear its ugly head. My boys go to a charter school so they have to wear uniforms. I think it's an amazing idea. Nobody gets judged for what they wear. It is also easier to pick out your school clothes in the morning.

In more important news: Our cat has been keeping us up at night with his snoring. As he gets older it just gets louder. We are thinking about getting him that strip you put over your nose.

Hiking the Himalayas
with a Cane

As a 20-year veteran in the financial industry, I've been trained, repeatedly, on how to design a retirement financial plan. I've come to the conclusion that many of the assumptions present in generic planning software are inaccurate. One common variable which nearly every planning tool emphasizes is the effect of inflation.

Most tools assume a 3 percent inflation rate throughout your retired years. If you do the math, that means that a gallon of milk which costs $5 now, will cost $10 twenty-four years from now.

While a 3 percent inflation rate is a reasonable assumption, it can really throw a wrench in most retirement scenarios. It stands to reason that if your monthly budget is presently $4000, you can expect for it to be $8000 a quarter century from now.

A little scary, isn't it? Maybe you should just sit on all of your savings as long as possible so that inflation doesn't ruin you. You don't want to spend your nineties living in a cardboard box behind a gas station.

Luckily, I have great news. The fear of inflation is a bunch of B.S. Or more accurately, the underlying assumptions in these calculations are missing one enormously important factor:

You will spend significantly less money in your eighties and nineties than you will in your sixties and seventies.

The U.S. Bureau of Labor Statistics found that retirees between the age of 65 and 74 spend 35 percent more money than retirees older than 75. The Government Accountability Office found that Americans spend 41 percent less in their early seventies compared with their late forties. [15]

How can this be?

1. You pay off your mortgage. This is an important variable to consider when designing a retirement budget. If your $1200 mortgage payment is going to end in six years, you need to account for that reduction in required monthly funds.

2. You will spend less on clothing, travel, gas, food, and entertainment. That doesn't mean you don't travel or go out to eat. Think about it—you won't have to buy a new work wardrobe every year or so. You won't have to pay for your kids to travel with you (if you have them). You'll still go out, but you may go out less.

3. You will not be buying a new car every few years. Hopefully, in the next ten years there are more public transportation options anyway, so all of us can stop buying a new car every few years!

4. Medical expenses generally do not increase until the end-of-life stage, at which point there can be a small spike in spending. Remember that 90 percent of retirees in America spend less than $2,000 a year on medical expenses while on Medicare.

5. Social Security accounts for inflation. Another key factor to remember is that your Social Security payments will grow with inflation. Social Security increases are based on the Consumer Price Index (or CPI).

Let's say Bobby Biggins retired 25 years ago with a monthly Social Security benefit of $1,000. Today that same monthly benefit would total $1,755.

For 2021, a 1.3 percent increase has been announced. For those of you receiving Social Security, you will see the increase this month. If you have yet to take Social Security, the 1.3 percent is still added to your future benefit.

So, to review, as you get older, inflation will increase the costs of goods and services, but this increase is offset by the natural reduction in spending as you age. Social Security will take inflation into account when determining your monthly benefit.

So what does all of this mean? For many of you, you may be able to spend more money earlier in your retirement.

Don't let the online retirement calculators fool you. You may be in much better long-term shape than you realize.

Family Update

My oldest son, Chris, is REALLY into reading. He just got into the Percy Jackson series. He would rather read than play on an iPad. That is truly extraordinary. Some of those books are 500 pages long. He has his own little nook in his room with a bean bag and a small table with a lamp. It's quite cozy. We always know where to find him.

To sign up for future newsletters
OR
To do your own plan online
(based on my beliefs)

Go to:
www.StopLivingScared.com
or call 941-556-6307

---

15. Retiring Soon? You May Spend a Lot Less Than You Think Less Than You Think

A CRASH COURSE ON
MARKET CRASHES

D id you know that most "normal" investors actually lost much less money during market "crashes" than the media reports?

I've been doing some historical digging and I've discovered some shocking truths. I hear a lot of horror stories about how much money people have lost during past crashes. You never know! You might be next! Get ready to live in on skid row!

The markets have had five significant crashes in the past 100 years. The Great Depression (1929)

- World War II (1939)
- Oil Embargo/Nixon Resignation (1973)
- The Dot Com/Technology Bubble (2000)
- The Great Recession/Real Estate Bubble (2008)

It may come as a surprise to many of you that there were decades-long periods without any major ''corrections'' in the markets. But I want to point out another interesting statistical curiosity.

Crashes typically cause short-term damage.

Allow me to explain through an analogy. If you invested all of your money at the beginning of 1929,1940, 1973, 2000, or 2008, you would have had a bad time. But in the real world, you generally don't suddenly invest all of your money at once. It is a gradual process as you save money and contribute to retirement accounts over many years. We need to look at the years preceding the crashes to get a true sense of how damaging they were to real people's financial lives.

Let's start with the years preceding the Great Depression.

- 1926: +11.6 percent
- 1927: +37.5 percent
- 1928: +43.6 percent

This means that if you had $100,000 invested in 1925, you saw it grow to $220,000 by the time the markets faltered. Over the next four years, your value dropped to $80,000. The markets then skyrocketed upwards again. By the end of 1936 your account was worth $241,000.

This means that over ten years (1925-1935) your investment in the S&P 500 would have increased from $100,000 to $241,000. That's an increase of 141 percent.

This was during the worst downturn in the history of the stock market.

The World War II crash saw a similar phenomenon. From 1935-1945 (with the markets dropping significantly in 1937, 1940, and 1941) your $100,000 investment would have turned into $242,000. How?

- 1936 had a 34 percent return.
- 1938: 31 percent
- 1942: 20 percent
- 1943: 26 percent
- 1944: 20 percent
- 1945: 36 percent

Who cares if you had a few bad years in between?

The years preceding and following the crash in 1973-74? Same thing. If you invested money from 1970 to 1980 (with the markets dropping 40 percent during the downturn), your $100,000 turned into $170,000.

The years leading up to the Dot Com Bubble in the early 2000s is the best example of this concept. The 1990s was the best decade the markets had ever seen. Your $100,000 investment turned into a whopping $530,000 during the 90s. Did you lose 40 percent from 2000-2002? Yes. But you would have still been WAY ahead.

Lastly, the crash nearest and dearest to our hearts; the real estate bubble was possibly the worst economic event since the Great Depression. But the 37 percent lost in 2008 was mitigated by solid returns before and after. If you invested $100,000 in 2005, today it would be worth $428,000.

I think you get my point by now. Stock market crashes do not occur in a vacuum. We need to look at returns before and after to get a better understanding of the true cost of downturns.

What does all of this mean for you?

Keep calm and carry on.

Family Update

My kids are now really into Monopoly. They haven't the faintest idea how the actual rules work. It's quite comical to watch them playing their version of the game. There is almost always an argument over who gets to be the banker.

My son Jesse was furious this morning when he didn't get to be the banker, but I told him, "You have to be 8-years-old to be banker."

He seemed pretty satisfied with that answer.

"Help" is not a Four Letter Word

My wife fought breast cancer five years ago. As you can imagine, we learned a lot about a lot of facets of life. She had great doctors, the surgery was grueling, but overall she completed the "process" of battling the disease alive and well. That isn't the part of the experience that surprised us the most.

What surprised us was all the help.

When you face a life-threatening illness (with four very young children) certain thoughts run through your mind. "How are we going to make it through this?"

We have some family down here, but they could only do so much. Somehow, we had to balance my wife's care, and the rest she needed, with the very real-life demands of raising four children.

Then something amazing happened.

People came out of the woodwork to help us. While some were friends before the illness, most were mere acquaintances. Maybe someone we met once or twice. Sometimes we were served by people who didn't even know us, but knew we were in a time of need.

It was an incredible experience. You don't know what support is there until you really need it.

So what's my point? Hardship faced alone is suffering. Hardship faced with help is still hard, but it is easier.

I watch people refuse help a lot.

On one occasion, a woman--we'll call her Debbie—was sitting with me in my office and said, "I poured my life into my kids. I wanted them to be productive, happy adults. I sacrificed so much for their well-being, I guess I neglected myself. I have almost no savings. I'm 68 years old. There aren't many jobs available to me. I'm still renting my place. I have no place to go."

Then she said, "At least my kids are all doing well. They seem happy, they all have good jobs and families. In fact, my oldest suggested that they convert the second floor of the garage into a mother-in-law suite. But I can't do that to my kids. Do they really want their mother getting in the way of things?"

This woman was willing to suffer alone rather than accept help from her daughter, literally one of her closest relationships on Earth. She was also going to miss out on the joyful experience of living near her grandchildren, and the amazing blessing of gratitude when you receive help freely given.

Most people are not providers throughout their lives. Sometimes you have to be okay with being the receiver, rather than the giver. The world is filled with caretakers, ready and eager to help. During my wife's battle with cancer, we realized that many people in the world are givers. They move through the world actively looking for people in need. And when they find someone they spring into action.

Why, then, do we assume nobody is willing to help? Why do we feel embarrassed and ashamed when we are unable to be the provider? There are people waiting to help you. There is no shame in asking for help. Let the helpers do their job.

During my wife's trials, we found that many other people with cancer did not get nearly as much help and support. Why? I think one reason is because people are so ashamed to need help that they won't ever ask for it.

When you are in need, you have to go out there, swallow your fear, and tell people.

Talk to your family, your friends, your church. Get your story out there. Few people will judge you, and you won't believe the helpers that start coming out from the woodwork. If you try to go it alone, you will struggle.

And let's go back to Debbie. Were Debbie's kids upset that their Mom was "coming home?" Doubtful. Her daughter had three kids of her own. She was probably desperate for help. Who cares if Mom doesn't have any money? That's not what Mom is about. Mom sacrificed her whole life for her children. Her eldest was probably happy and grateful she could help her mother in return.

Repeat after me: You are not how much money you make. Your value, to your family, friends, community, is not conditional on whether or not you are paying your own way.

My wife comes from the Thai culture, and in that society it is assumed that as people get older, younger generations are there to help. It would be seen as blasphemy to turn away a family member in need. Almost every culture in the world has functioned this way for hundreds of years.

What a liberating concept! All those helpers out there are just waiting for someone like you to express a need. Let them do what they do best. Otherwise the helpers of this world have nothing to do.

Family Update

The kids are spending a week with Grammy and Pop in Pittsburgh. It is the one week a year without kids. My wife and I plan to travel a bit. Last year, by day four, we missed the kids so much we wanted them to come home.

Grammy takes the kids out of the house at least once a day to expel some energy. Here are some planned activities.

1. Go to a pet store and look at the animals.
2. Miniature golf.
3. Visit a local farm and pick strawberries.
4. Go to Target to buy Legos.
5. Feed ducks at the local pond.
6. Visit Aunt Ruthie and Aunt Jeanie.

Sounds like a full week to me.

What Happened if you Invested Your Money in the *1800's*?

This week we are going to talk about distant history. We are going waaaaaay back.

I often talk about how, in the past 100 years, the stock and bond markets have shown remarkable consistency. The patterns they exhibit are so clear that it's impossible to ignore.

But let's dig deeper. Maybe this past century was an anomaly. What about the 1800s?

That's right, we are going back to the days of the Louisiana Purchase and the Civil war.

I have spoken at great length in the past about how stocks had returned an average of 10 percent during the 20th century, but what about the 19th century?

Now remember, the light bulb wasn't invented until 1879 and the leading cause of death in 1900 was tuberculosis.

So, how did the stock market hold up? We have good data from Dr. Jeremy Siegel who wrote the fantastic book, Stocks for the Long Run. His data shows that from 1801-1900 the stock market returned an average of 6.51 percent.

At first glance that appears to be a little disappointing, especially considering that from 1901-2000 the stock market returned an average of 9.89 percent.

But all is not as straight-forward as it seems. You see, in the 1800s the country saw very little inflation. In fact, something that cost $1 in the year 1800, cost a little less than a dollar one-hundred years later in 1900.

That means that, after inflation, stocks from 1800-1900 returned 6.76 percent. And from 1900-2000, after inflation, the stock market returned a real return of 6.45 percent. You need to subtract out inflation from stock returns to get the real return—the amount of purchasing power your money has grown after inflation.

What is the takeaway? Here's mine:

History really does repeat itself. The stock market, after inflation, has had a similar average return for over 200 *years*.

Stop. Go back. Read that again.

Going forward, while no one can guarantee what will happen, don't you want to base your financial decisions on an incredibly consistent pattern that has persisted for centuries?

If you invest in a diversified portfolio of stocks and bonds you are giving yourself the best chance, statistically, to succeed. Investments such as gold, commodities, certificates of deposit, and currencies can have wild and inconsistent returns. Don't make this more complicated than it is!

Family Update

My wife, daughter and middle son visited New York City for the weekend. The first thing my daughter said upon arrival was, "Why would anyone want to live here?" (I agree)

My son learned the proper way to eat New York style pizza, they rode the subway, and even saw the Broadway play "Hamilton."

They found one of the biggest problems was finding bathrooms. I noticed the same thing when I visited. Do New Yorkers know of secret spots that are hidden from us lowly tourists?

LOSING MONEY BY NOT
LOSING MONEY

In the past week I have had three separate people say the same thing to me. Paraphrasing a bit, it went something like this: "I kept my money in cash since the 2008 crash because while I understood that I wasn't going to make any money, at least I wasn't going to *lose* any."

After the first person told me this, I thought to myself, "I guess that is reasonable. At least they feel safe and secure."

After the second person, I thought to myself, "I guess that makes sense, but is this really a rationale and logical way to approach this situation?"

After the third person, I thought to myself, "But you ARE losing money. You ARE losing money!"

You are losing money in three different ways.

While you may be eliminating market risk, there are other risks at play here. Inflation risk is a very real issue. If inflation is increasing the price of goods and services by 3 percent per year and your money is making 1 percent per year, you are losing 2 percent per year of purchasing power.

You are also exposing yourself to opportunity risk. If a balanced portfolio of stocks and bonds were to return 10 percent, you just LOST 10 percent. Just because you didn't see a red "minus" next to your account number, doesn't mean you didn't lose money.

The biggest risk you face in retirement is "longevity risk" which is the risk that you are going to live much longer than you expected. Your money needs to keep growing, period. You can't rely on a two percent CD.

Here is a real gut punch to anyone who moved their money to cash in 2008. $100,000 invested in the stock market in early 2009 is now worth $412,000. That means you LOST $312,000. There is no other way to look at it. That is a much larger loss than the actual crash itself.

It is extremely difficult to get my clients to view things this way, but it might be the most important mathematical concept in this book. "Staying safe" does not mean you will protect yourself from losing money.

Ironically, if your money is "safely" not working for you during your retired years, you could be dramatically increasing your chances of running out of money.

That's right. People who are trying to protect themselves from running out of money might run out of money by trying to protect themselves from running out of money.

Family Update

My son, Alex, who tends to have intense, fleeting interests, planted some sunflower seeds. Sunflowers grow incredibly quickly. I've seen my him peering at his sunflower plants at 7:00 AM as the sun is rising. "I can't believe that flower came from that seed," he commented. The sunflowers are about one inch now, but before you know it we will have flowers and vegetables coming out of our ears. This is assuming, of course, that gardening keeps everyone's attention. These phases usually don't.

How we Advisors get Paid

Broker or registered representation? Investment Advisor Representative or Fiduciary?

Whew! Why does this have to be so complicated?

Whenever you choose to work with a financial advisor they fall into one of two camps: brokers and fiduciaries. Most people don't know the difference, but it is important that you do!

Let's start with broker relationships. Brokers are paid transactionally. If you are working with a broker and they put you into some sort of financial product, they are paid via a commission. If they move your money to another spot later down the road, they get paid again. It's transactional.

In my personal experience, when working with a broker, people can't help but think, "Sure, Bob seems like a nice guy and he certainly knows what he is doing, BUT…. is he using this particular product because he's getting paid more? Is there some sort of financial kickback, lurking in the background, which helped him make his decision?"

In addition, whenever a broker suggests a change to an investment strategy you might say to yourself, "Is he doing this so that he can get paid again? Or is this actually in my best interest?"

Brokers are held to a "suitability standard" which means they are "required to implement an investment strategy that meets the objectives of the investor." Notice that it doesn't say, "Brokers have to put you in the absolute best investments for your situation."

It only says that it must at least loosely satisfy what you are looking for.

Am I splitting hairs? Let's take a look at how fiduciaries must operate under the legal standard: "…the fiduciary standard simply means that the advisor puts their clients' interests above their own. For example, the advisor is prohibited from making trades that may result in higher commissions for the advisor or his or her investment firm."

The other big difference is how a fiduciary gets paid. An advisor entering into a fiduciary arrangement with a client is not allowed to receive commissions. Their compensation is not transactional. Generally, fiduciaries are paid an advisory fee (usually around a 1 percent annual fee) which fosters a professional, long-term relationship versus a limited, transaction-oriented one.

How does the 1 percent fee work? Let's say at the end of the year, you look at your portfolio's performance and you see an 8 percent gain. In reality, the portfolio returned 9 percent. Most advisors bill (directly from the account) .25 percent each quarter to total the 1 percent. The fees are completely transparent and listed on your statement.

With a broker, it is difficult to determine their compensation, which usually consists of hidden fees that are difficult to translate. Why is this important? Because, while working with a fiduciary, you never have to ask yourself, "Why is my advisor choosing this investment vs. that investment? Why is my advisor making trades in my account? Why is my advisor moving my money from one place to another?"

Within a fiduciary relationship, you are inherently on the same team. When you do better, they do better. The more your money grows, the more they make (the 1 percent fee is on a larger account value).

I'm not saying everyone needs to be working with a fiduciary. Broker relationships can still be beneficial to some people. But in my own personal experience, client relationships, where I am operating as a fiduciary, seem to be the most productive and meaningful. So how do you find out if your advisor is acting in a fiduciary capacity? Just ask them!

Family Update

We are currently visiting my Mom and Dad. The weather in Pittsburgh is perfect. My daughter and Grammy adore each other. They are at each other's side 24/7. They even sleep in the same bed. My youngest son loves to play in the basement (none of those in Florida). It has ping pong, darts, and lots of room to mess around.

My oldest son's favorite part is the shuffleboard. My parents installed a regulation shuffleboard court in their backyard. Sounds like a party to me!

Don't try to Outsmart
the Markets

I am often asked, "Can't we just take the money out of our portfolio when the markets are going down, and then put the money back in, right when it hits the bottom?"

While this may sound like a reasonable plan, in reality it is absolutely impossible to actually accomplish.

No one knows when the market will "hit bottom." Anyone that says they can time the market is either lying or delusional.

The perils of market timing have been quantified by Dalbar, a highly-regarded financial services research firm.

In a study they conducted from 1995-2014, they looked at what various investments actually returned vs. what average investors actually made. From 1995-2014 (averages):

- Stocks: +9.9%
- Bonds: +6.2%
- Int'l Stocks: +5.0%
- The Average Investor: +2.5%
- Inflation: 2.3%

That means that the average investor only captured about one quarter of the total return of the stock market. The primary issue the average investor faced? You guessed it—market timing. Investors were switching in and out of funds at inopportune times.

Human beings are emotional creatures. Everyone knows that you should "buy low and sell high" but very few people actually do it. People panic. People make irrational decisions.

You need a plan and you need to stick to it. Stop thinking you can outsmart the markets.

You can't.

Family Update

My 8-year-old son was a hot dog for Halloween and since then he has become quite attached to his costume. Last week my family went to an arcade in Orlando where he wore his outfit. People were coming up to him and asking, "Why are you dressed as a hot dog?" And he would reply, "I like being a hot dog."

He later told me he likes being a hot dog because "anyone who looks at me either smiles or laughs." What a cool kid.

Most of these crops are planted from seed. As my boys were picking out seed packets at Lowe's my youngest got all excited when he saw the cucumber seed packet. He cried out, "Look, we can grow a pickle bush!

It Doesn't Matter if you Die

S am and Sarah Mayer, ages 83 and 85, go to visit a local financial advisor.

"Sonny boy," Sarah quips, "We have $500,000 in the bank and it's making basically nothing.

We were wondering if we should invest it in something."

"Well," he remarked, "You guys are old as dirt. I guess we can't put you into anything too risky."

"Old! We don't even buy green bananas anymore," she laughed.

"The standard rule is that you should subtract your age from 100 and that is how much you should put in the stock market," the advisor informed them.

"So I guess we might want to consider putting 15% in the stock market and the rest into very conservative government bonds and money markets. Maybe even in some fixed annuities."

Sam nodded. "Makes sense to us. We certainly don't have time for our money to recover if the stock market crashes. In fact, we are actually able to save money each month now. We are spending less than our Social Security and pensions. So we can probably put more money into this each month and make it grow even more!"

Sarah added, "We're saving this money for our dear grandson anyway. If we don't need it, we figure we can bless him with it. He had three great-grandkids for us!"

So Sam and Sarah put their money in this ultra-conservative portfolio and went home... never realizing their poor decision.

This anecdote outlines a concept I've battled for years — that as you get older, you need to become more and more conservative with your investments because you "don't have enough time to make it back."

Not only do I think this is a ridiculous idea, but the results can be incredibly expensive.

Let's think about why this thinking is so faulty.

Markets recover very quickly. Even if they put 100% of their money in the stock market (which they shouldn't), historically, recovery times have never been more than 3 or 4 years.

So this whole concept of "We don't have time for this to recover" is assuming both of them will die in the next three or four years.

Granted, that is possible. This is why 100% in the stock market is not a good idea, either.

Now, let's look at someone who invests 70% of their money in stocks and 30% in bonds. Remember that when stocks go down, bonds go up. In the past 50 years, the worst return would have been from 2008, where you would have lost 24%. Certainly not fun, but it's not like you went bankrupt. With this portfolio you would have made all of the money back in a little over *one year*.

Quick note: The second worst return of this portfolio over the past fifty years was in 2001 where you would have lost 12% and the third worst was 4% in 1976.

Think about that for a second. *In fifty years you would have lost a noticeable amount of money* **two times!**

"But Dave, what happens if you need a bunch of money for medical expenses!"

I've spoken at length about how huge medical expenses just do not happen as long as you are on Medicare. The only real scare is a nursing home. You would have to start drawing down this money. But strategically all you need to do is use the money from the bond portion of the portfolio first (which is up if the markets are down). By the time your bonds run out, the stock market will have more than recovered.

But here is the main thrust of my argument. There is a 95% chance that they will never use the money. There is probably a 1% chance they use all of it. They're pretty long in the tooth. They are happy with their lifestyle. They don't want more stuff. Money doesn't mean much to them. Their budget is not going to increase.

So if you think about it, what is this money for? In other words, whose money is this *really?*

It's their grandson's. There is a 90% chance he will get most, if not all, of the money. So what does this mean?

They need to invest the money as their grandson would.

It's as if the advisor sat down with their grandson directly and advised him on a portfolio. A lot of professionals in my industry would look upon this as blasphemy, but with twenty years of experience I have absolutely no doubt this is the appropriate strategy.

By Sam and Sarah investing the money according to their age, they are taking money away from their grandson. Probably a lot of money.

Let's say this conversation happened ten years ago in 2011 and Sam and Sarah made it all the way to 2021.

If they had invested $500,000 in 15% stocks and 85% bonds, the current account balance would stand at around $900,000. Not bad! Certainly better than getting .1% at the bank.

But what if they used the 70% stock/30% bond mix? In 2021, the grand total reached $1,500,000.

Oops. I'm sure Sam and Sarah's grandson is grateful and will do great things with his $900,000. But the point is, they could have made him a millionaire.

I strongly believe that anyone, regardless of age, should have at least 60-70% of their money in the stock market.

The only time that it doesn't make sense is if you are sure you are going to spend the money in the next five years. Most seniors do not have those plans.

Don't buy into the traditional thinking. It's a bunch of hooey. You need to invest your money based on what it is for, not your age.

Family Update

My youngest son Jesse (age 8) had his first sleepover. I have such incredibly fond memories of sleepovers. You get to hang out, and when it is time for bed you can fake that you're sleeping and then talk and giggle in the dark.

That is exactly what happened with Jesse. The next day he was a crabby mess.

Are you Going to Have an Awesome Retirement?

These TEN QUESTIONS will let you know your level of retirement awesomeness.

(Add up all the times you answer "yes")

1. I know how much money I spend each month (on average). YES/NO

2. I have spent time planning for the best age to begin receiving Social Security benefits. YES/NO

3. I make it a point to NOT watch any of the 24/7 financial news channels. YES/NO

4. My retirement savings is invested in a diversified portfolio of stocks and bonds, with at least half of the money in stocks. YES/NO

5. I understand that once enrolled in Medicare and a Medicare supplement, the maximum out-of-pocket expense for any given year is less than $10,000. YES/NO

6. I know how much I will need to pay in federal taxes per year once retired. YES/NO

7. I believe that the money I have saved for retirement is meant to be spent and enjoyed during my retired years. YES/NO

8. I am going to start taking out a reasonable amount of money from my retirement accounts each month once retired. YES/NO

9. I am going to stop focusing on *saving* money once I am retired. YES/NO

10. I am going to (or already have) put careful thought, time and effort into planning in my retirement years for both my financial and personal life. YES/NO

Results

Please add up the number of times you answered "yes."

0-3 OH MY! You are in serious danger of giving yourself unnecessary grief in retirement. Without planning and education, you might end up living a life fearing the unknown. Consider making the unknown, known. You will almost certainly reduce anxiety and increase awesomeness.

4-7 Keep Going! You are on the right track. There are just a few more misconceptions you may have in your brain. Keep reading this book and others like it to replace misconceptions with facts.

8-10 You've Arrived! You get to enjoy your retired years understanding the parameters by which you can live your life. You've found the perfect balance between spending too much money and spending too little. You get to enjoy the fruits of your labor. Your days will be filled with bountiful awesomeness.

Family Update

My 14-year-old daughter had a sleepover with five other girls this weekend. It was non-stop laughter and excitement. Dad made sure no boys snuck into the equation. I sat on a rocking chair with a shotgun in my lap. (I'm just kidding)

We have a trampoline in our back yard and the girls decided that they were all going to sleep out there. They created a tent-like structure using sheets. I must be getting old, but sleeping outside on a trampoline sounds terrible.

Don't be Like Joe

H ere's a story about two guys named Joe and Frank.

They both retired 25 years ago (1995) at age 65 with $1,000,000 in savings. Two different people in two different parts of the country except for one big difference—Joe made his decisions based on fear, and Frank based his decisions on realistic expectations.

When Joe retired he went to the local bank and said, "I'm retired now, I can't afford to lose anything. I want to put all my money in a money market." In 1995 money markets were paying an average of 3.9 percent, and Joe felt pretty good about that. Joe was fearful. "I don't want to spend any of this money unless I HAVE to. I know my wife has been bothering me about getting a new kitchen, and I would love to visit the grandkids in Rhode Island, but… I'm not making a salary anymore. I have to be very careful with this."

Over the next 25 years Joe scrimped and saved; he never took anything out of his savings beyond a few thousand dollars here and there. When he died in 2020, there was quite a bit of money still there. Over 25 years of compounding interest inside the money market account had turned his $1,000,000 into $1,800,000. Joe and his wife never actually got to enjoy any of his savings, but at least they didn't run out of money, right?

Now Frank looked at things completely differently. "I've worked my whole life so that I could enjoy the fruits of my labor in retirement. We are going to put a pool in the backyard. Both Mary and I love to swim and it will keep us active and healthy. We are going to travel as much as we can, especially in our sixties and seventies."

Frank went to a local advisor and said, "I want to invest in a diversified portfolio of stocks and bonds. I want my money to keep working for me even though I am no longer making a salary."

So Frank put 60 percent of his savings into stocks and 40 percent into bonds– a very common portfolio asset mix. Frank then started taking out $70,000 a year from his portfolio; or 7 percent of the original value. His friends called him crazy. "You are too old for investing," they would say. "You are going to run out of money!"

So Frank spent the $70,000 each year on things that made him and his wife happy. They spent an entire month in Australia. They traveled up north for each of their grandkids' birthdays. Frank even bought himself a 1969 cherry red Chevy Camaro.

When Frank died in 2020 his kids gathered and looked at his investment statement. How much money did Frank have left over in 2020? He had taken out $1,750,000 over those 25 years. His kids smiled at each other as they remembered all the crazy adventures their parents had with that money.

At Frank's death $3,480,000 remained. He started with $1,000,000, took out $1,750,000, and ended up with over three times the amount he started with. He also ended up with twice as much as Joe.

The Moral of the Story: Life is meant to be lived!

Other valuable lessons:

You may be able to spend more money each month than you realize. Being "safe" with your money may not actually be safe at all!

A well-diversified and balanced portfolio of stocks and bonds is a powerful wealth creation tool.

Family Update

As the kids find more ways to entertain themselves, they need to continue getting more creative. Their latest adventure involves digging a huge hole in the backyard. They're attempting to create an underground fortress. This takes some serious digging.

Their goal is to make it eight feet deep and six feet wide. Right now it's about six inches deep. I'm guessing they may discover a new activity before their bunker is complete.

Worst Case Scenario

New York University has some fantastic long-term historical financial data1. As always, I want to delve into the world of data, statistics, history and probability. It may sound boring, but it's not!

I am constantly battling against the concept that investing is unpredictable and risky. This week we are going to look at what would have happened, historically speaking, to someone with a portfolio of 50/50 stocks/bonds.

Why? I want to show you that your concept of volatility may be out of whack. Most people I meet with believe that, in any given year, a balanced and diversified portfolio of stocks and bonds might lose 50 percent or more.

Hmmm … is that true?

Let's look at the time period stretching from 1940 until 2020. During that 80 year stretch, what was the worst single year result of a 50/50 stocks/bonds portfolio?

The worst year? 1974. The combination of a worldwide oil embargo and the resignation of Richard Nixon made for a really bad year in the financial markets.

In 1974 you would have lost 12 percent. The stock market was down 26 percent and the bond market was up 2 percent. If you had $100,000 in your 50/50 split portfolio, half of it would have lost $13,000 and the other half would have made $1,000. During that year, your portfolio would have dropped from $100,000 to $88,000. That was the WORST.

Here is every year the stock market has gone down since 1940 combined with what the bond market did that same year.

YEAR	STOCKS (S&P 500 INDEX)	BONDS (10 YEAR T. BOND)	TOTAL
1940	-11%	5.4%	-5.6%
1941	-13%	-2%	-15%
1946	-8.4%	3%	-5.4%
1953	-1.2%	4%	+2.8%
1957	-10.5%	6.8%	-3.7%
1962	-8.8%	5.7%	-3.1%
1969	-8.2%	-5%	-13.2%
1973	-14.3%	3.6%	-10.6%
1974	-26%	2%	-24%
1977	-7%	1.3%	-5.7%
1981	-4.7%	8.2%	+3.5%
1990	-3%	6.2%	+3.2%
2000	-9%	16.6%	+7.6%
2001	-12%	5.5%	-6.5%
2002	-22%	15%	-7%
2008	-37%	20%	-17%
2018	-4.2%	0%	-4.2%

Of course, I can't guarantee what will happen in the future. But, these patterns are hard to ignore.

Takeaways

Losing 50 percent of the value of your diversified investment portfolio is not a realistic expectation.

A "balanced" portfolio can oftentimes be pictured as a "see-saw."

---

16. Source: (1) http://pages.stern.nyu.edu/~adamodar/New_Home_Page/datafile/histretSP.

Stocks go down, bonds go up.

Over this period, the stock market was down 16 out of 76 years. It was down by more than 15 percent only three times.

A balanced, diversified portfolio of stocks and bonds is a remarkably powerful way to grow your money. You are not speculating. You are investing.[16]

Family Update

There is a passionate argument happening at my house. We are arguing over the answer to this question:

Is a hot dog a sandwich?

There are two schools of thought.

A hot dog is a sandwich because it has bread on both sides and meat in the middle. In a restaurant, if you looked at the menu, under the "sandwiches" section, that is where they would list "hot dog."

But there is a flip side to this argument.

A hot dog is NOT a sandwich.

The bun is connected together, instead of two separate slices of bread. It certainly does not fit the standard category of sandwich. If you asked someone for a sandwich and they gave you a hot dog, you would probably say, "Why are you giving me a hot dog? I wanted a sandwich."

Banks Going out of Business?

H ere's a good question:

What happens if I have my mutual funds and investments with a bank, and the bank goes bankrupt? (JP Morgan Chase, BofA, Merrill Lynch, etc.)

I've had several people express this concern to me over the past couple weeks, so let's take a look.

Whenever you buy a stock or bond or mutual fund, that investment has to be "held" somewhere. Back in the good old days, many people would actually hold stock certificates inside a safe in their house.

Nowadays, with modern technology, stocks and bonds are held electronically at a "custodian." A custodian is simply a financial institution that holds your investments.

So what happens if the custodian goes bankrupt? First of all, this is an extremely rare occurrence. In 2008, when Lehman Brothers went bankrupt, JP Morgan Chase purchased them and took over the custodial responsibilities. Not a single account holder lost a penny due to the bankruptcy of the custodian. It simply meant that JP Morgan Chase started to hold the stocks and bonds instead of Lehman Brothers.

But what you really need to know is the following: whoever is holding your investments has no financial claim to your money. Your assets are held separately from the bank's assets.

For most of you who work with me, you know that we employ TD Ameritrade. This particular bank holds over a trillion dollars in client assets.

If TD Ameritrade comes out tomorrow and says they are going bankrupt, what happens to your money?

Let me answer that question, by asking another question. Let's say you purchase 100 shares of Disney stock, and you request the actual paper stock certificates, and you put those certificates in a safety deposit box at a local bank. If that bank went bankrupt, would you lose your stock certificates?

Absolutely not. You would go to the now-bankrupt bank, open up your safety deposit box, and take your stock certificates.

The same thing applies to you and your investments now.

There are actually several additional layers of safeguards for consumers, including SIPC insurance. So if you are concerned about the bank holding your investments, please stop. There is nothing to worry about.

Family Update

My daughter stopped baking me brownies. Which is good for my waistline. But I went up to her room the other night and she has a HUGE stash of candy in her room. I mean, HUGE. Oreos, Sour Patch Kids, chocolate bars, potato chips, Snickers.... She somehow convinced our babysitter to take her to Target and I guess she got herself a secret bunker of food.

BUYING MARIJUANA WITH BITCOIN

Confucius, 2,500 years ago, announced, "Life is really simple, but we insist on making it complicated."

And now, when it comes to investing while retired, it appears many retirees are making the exact same mistake.

While I can't guarantee what will happen in the future, I can't help but notice a pretty remarkable history of success when it comes to good, old-fashioned stocks and bonds. It seems we human beings can't help but try to find the "next best thing."

Since 1975, if you look over 20-year periods, bonds have always returned an average of at least five percent. I can go back all the way to the year 1800 and show you similar results.

Since 1931, if you look over 20 year periods, stocks have always returned an average of at least seven percent. (In fact, the average over the past 100 years is nearly 10 percent.)

So why are we making this more complicated than it needs to be? Why are we trying to reinvent the wheel?

The wheel is not broken. At all.

During the course of my day-to-day business, I see a myriad of people just like you with portfolios filled with non-traditional investments.

Some Examples:

Marijuana Stocks: You were a product of the 60's. You would think there would be a huge demand, right? It's not as simple as that.

Problems: Mutual funds focused on the marijuana industry lost 70% in 2020. The industry is so new and there are so many unknowns. Believe it or not, there is an incredible oversupply of cannabis. Not to mention it is not even federally legal.

Bitcoin: I have no problem with Bitcoin. It could become a big player in the global financial markets. I have no idea. But the daily volatility is incredible. It is pure speculation. You are gambling. Collectibles: Want to stake your future on classic cars, coins, art, and jewelry? Then this is for you!

Problems: Uncertain pricing, forgeries, doesn't produce any income, high costs for storage, no consistent track record, no income, limited transparency, high commissions.

Venture Capital/Private Equity: Want to get in on the ground floor of a new business? Do you really like watching the TV show Shark Tank? Then this is for you!

Problems: Illiquid, highly speculative (you could lose all of your money), lack of transparency.

Currency Trading: Want to bet on what direction the dollar is going to trend in relation to the Euro? Have fun!

Problems: Zero sum game, no consistent track record, a short-term trading strategy with no academically provable benefit, wildly volatile.

Shorting the Market: Want to make money when the stock market goes down? Be my guest. But, remember, the stock market has been going up by an average of 10 percent over the past 200 years. It's kind of like betting on the Cleveland Browns to win the Super Bowl.

So what am I trying to say?

A diversified portfolio of stocks and bonds is a strategy with an incredibly long, consistent, and successful track record.

Don't make this more complicated than it is. Use the wheel. It works. It will get you where you want to be.

Family Update

School is here again. It's really stressful the first couple days, but then we get into a nice routine. The three boys all get to go to the same school, which is pretty cool. And so far my daughter Senay absolutely loves 7th grade. How many people can say that they have a 7th grade girl who loves school? Isn't that supposed to be a difficult time with bullies and hormones and various other transitions? I'm not going to jinx it. She sometimes comes home from school humming a tune.

Spending Money in a Down Market

Today I want to talk a little bit about withdrawing money from an investment portfolio that is not growing.

Faithful followers of the Retirement Revolution already know my core beliefs.

When you retire:

Invest the money in a diversified portfolio of stock and bonds (with at least half the money in stocks).

Begin spending five percent of your portfolio each year starting the very first year you retire.

At its core, the basic concept is this: Between now and the end of your life, if the above-referenced portfolio does NOT return an average of five percent it will be the first time in modern economic history where it has failed to do so.

In a sense, you are only spending the money that your money is making.

Now, this can sometimes get psychologically tricky during times of flat growth or even losses in the portfolio.

Let me (poorly) draw a couple of pictures to make my point.

In a perfect world, your experience with your portfolio spending plan would look like this:

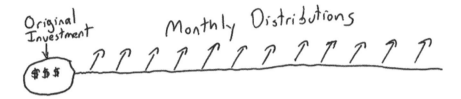

Wouldn't that be nice? Your principal would stay completely stable, and you would simply take the earnings each month. Unfortunately, that is not how this works.

Here is a more accurate representation of what your experience will probably look like.

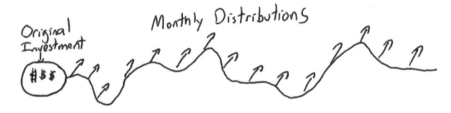

There will be times when it feels like you are taking money from an account that is going down. You will see your principal reducing as you are spending the money. For many people, this can cause mild to moderate heartburn.

Take an Alka-Seltzer. You are going to be okay.

But sometimes (like in the past few years) you might take out your five percent and see that the portfolio grows above and beyond your withdrawals. "This is great," you might think, "not only do I get to enjoy the money I'm withdrawing, but my account is actually *growing.*"

In order to get the most LIFE from your money, you need to come to terms with the fact that the markets do not move in a perfectly straight line. They may temporarily go down but they permanently go up. As Warren Buffett points out, in 1900 the Dow Jones was 66 points. As of this writing, the Dow Jones is trading at over 30,000.

Family Update

This is so funny to me.

My three boys went to Target and bought Christmas presents for each other. As they have never done anything like this before, it was very big deal.

Once at the store, we all needed separate carts as to not ruin the surprise. After we returned home, they quickly wrapped the presents and put them under the tree for Christmas morning.

By the end of that very night, the boys had already given each other their presents. They tried so hard. They just couldn't wait.

SOCIAL SECURITY IS NOT
GOING BROKE

The solvency of Social Security is, understandably, a hot topic. The program supplies the majority of retirement income to the majority of retirees. The fear that Social Security may disappear makes it even harder for Baby Boomers to spend a little bit of their savings once they retire.

Many people have the attitude of, "If Social Security goes bankrupt, I will need as much in savings as possible to survive. I better not spend a penny or I could be in big trouble if the system crumbles." To make matters worse, I have been seeing an increase in scary articles on the internet about Social Security going broke.

Why the increase? Because you click on the articles. News outlets are going to keep producing headlines that grab your attention. It doesn't really matter if the articles have any academic merit.

Here are some doozies:

- Social Security isn't going broke; it's already broke.
- Report: Social Security Will Bankrupt America Faster Than We Thought
- 5 Signs Social Security Is Going Insolvent

I want you to make your financial decisions based on the facts, not some random guy's opinion.

According to the annual trustee's report, Social Security is fully funded until 2034 at which point it will be 75 percent funded until

2093. Proactive steps are already being taken to keep the system afloat for as long as you are alive.

By increasing payroll taxes from 6.2 percent to 8.2 percent, the system would be 100 percent funded for 75 years.

Congress has already begun increasing the earnings limit on Social Security taxes. It has been increasing incrementally for years. In the year 2000, you had to pay payroll taxes on the first $76,000 of income. Today the limit is $128,400.

If Tom Brady makes $30 million dollars, he only has to pay Social Security tax on the first $128,400. There is serious discussion about abolishing this policy. It would super-charge revenues for the system.

Note: As of January, 2021, President Biden is proposing that people will need to pay this tax on all of their income.

There are several proposals to increase the retirement age to 70. But this would not apply to you.

Cutting Social Security benefits is absolute political suicide. Can you imagine the politician who comes out and says, "If elected I will cut your Social Security and your parents'?"

As Dwight Eisenhower once famously said, "Should any political party attempt to abolish Social Security…you would not hear of that party again in our political history."

Social Security is backed by the full faith of the U.S. government. What does this mean? The federal government has all kinds of ways to increase funding for any sort of program. Social Security is the financial bedrock for most people in this country. Cutting benefits would cause widespread bankruptcy, foreclosures, and other economic devastation. Social Security is one of the last programs the government will ever cut. It is just too important to the fabric of our society.

To summarize: You will get what your Social Security statement says that you are going to get. And you will get it for the rest of your life.

Don't let this common misconception sabotage your retirement. Be comforted by the fact that you don't need to obsessively save until your dying day because "you never know" if Social Security will still be there. It will be.

Family Update

My two youngest boys have made the most massive fort I have ever witnessed. They've been working on it for a week and they are very proud of themselves.

It spans the entire game room. It required chairs, sofas, twenty blankets and a LOT of duct tape.

There are two bedrooms, a living room, a dining room and they are working on the kitchen. Luckily the bathroom is the actual bathroom in the room.

Let Your Life pay Dividends

Let's say you have a diversified portfolio of stocks and bonds. Some of the money you make is from dividends and interest. Some of the money you make is capital growth (the value the stock or bond increases).

For example, the Coca-Cola Co. is currently paying around a three percent dividend. If you invest $100,000 into Coca-Cola stock, you will receive $3,000 in dividends during the year. Dividends are simply profits that companies give back to shareholders.

So, what happens if the Coca-Cola Co. has a huge drop in its share price? Let's say it loses 30 percent for example.

If your $100,000 in stock is now worth $70,000, how much money will you receive each year in dividends going forward?

The dividends would be 30 percent less, right? You would only get around $2,000 a year going forward, right?

Nope. You would continue to receive $3,000 a year. How is that possible? Dividends are not a function of stock price. They are set by the company's board of directors in a big, fancy boardroom.

Here's an educational analogy. Let's say you buy a rental property. You pay $100,000 for the house and you start receiving $1,000/mo in rent. What happens if another real estate bubble bursts and the value goes down? What happens if, when you go on Zillow to see the current value of your home, it says $70,000?

Do you start getting 30 percent less in rent? No. The rent doesn't change. The underlying asset may temporarily be worthless, but the rent doesn't change. You and the renter agreed on a rent payment; it does not automatically change based on the listed price of the home.

This is an absolutely essential concept to understand. Why? Because it should help insulate you from fear about the markets.

Many diversified income-oriented portfolios in the current economy could pay around a 3 percent dividend on stocks, and around a 3 percent yield on bonds. So no matter what happens to the share price of your stocks and bonds, that 3 percent keeps getting paid out. It is a huge buffer in volatile markets.

Can companies decrease dividends? Sure, but it is much more common for them to increase dividends. And, don't forget a diversified portfolio of stocks contains hundreds, if not thousands, of companies.

In 2020, dividends increased for U.S. stocks by 57 percent. In fact, 53 stocks in the S&P 500 have increased dividends every year, for 25 years. The Coca-Cola Company has increased dividends every year for 55 years. These stocks are often referred to as the Dividend Aristocrats.

My point is this: regardless of share price, your cash flow continues. Dividends and interest are powerful tools for retirement income creation. It is not all about the share price.

And now you know! And knowledge is power!

Family Update

My youngest son, Jesse, brought home a lima bean sprout about two months ago. We planted the little fella in the back yard and forgot all about it. Last week we discovered something incredible. That little sprout had grown and developed. In fact, hanging off the longest tendril was a single, perfect lima bean pod. I picked it and brought it to Jesse. I've never seen his eyes get so big. It was adorable. He named it Larry the Lima Bean.

To sign up for future newsletters
OR
To do your own plan online
(based on my beliefs)

Go to:
www.StopLivingScared.com
or call 941-556-6307

Five Retirement Savings tips for Your Kids

C oncerned your kids are not properly preparing for retirement? You may have a good reason. According to a Business Insider website article, "Only half of Gen Xers have a retirement account, and that's a catastrophe in the making" only 36 percent of Gen X is actively saving for retirement. (Millennials, on the other hand, seem to be starting retirement saving earlier and are more actively saving.)

With the Thanksgiving holiday approaching, now is as good a time as ever to broach the subject. Let me give you a few facts and insights to pass with the mashed potatoes. I usually expound on how many retiring Baby Boomers are worrying themselves sick about running out of money. I discuss how many retirees are in much better shape than they realize. I reveal ways how you can get the most life out of your money. I encourage you to empower yourselves to live the retirement you deserve.

But let's also make sure your kids will be financially prepared for their retired years. Remember, you never stop being a parent.

5 Tips to Give Your Kids About Saving for Retirement

1. Pay yourself first. This simply means that the money you are saving should come automatically out of your paycheck or bank account. Do not promise yourself that you will save whatever is left over at the end of the month. It does not work. At all.

2. Give until it hurts. Maybe saving $100 a month sounds reasonable and comfortable. I strongly suggest you start saving $200 or even $500 per month. Choose a number that feels a little scary and uncomfortable. You can always lower the amount if it ends up being too much.

Most people adjust quickly to their new savings plan and find they are able to save more than they first thought. In my experience, few people increase their contribution once they start.

3. Invest into a 401(k) or IRA. These accounts give you a tax deduction upfront and defer taxation until you withdraw the money. In addition, by using a retirement account the money is more "tied up" than normal savings. This might make you hesitate to use money from your retirement accounts for non-retirement reasons. Another great reason to invest in a 401(k) is matching. Many companies will match their employees' retirement contributions, up to a certain point. Don't throw away free retirement money.

4. Invest 100 percent of the money in the stock market. Don't make this more complicated than it is. We are talking loooooong term investing here. Stocks have been returning an average of 10 percent over any meaningful time period throughout economic history.

5. Understand the power of compounding interest. It doesn't especially matter how much you save, but for how long you save it. The table below assumes somebody invests $100 per month into a 401(k) or IRA and places 100 percent of the money into the stock market.

AGE SAVING BEGINS	IF YOU SAVE $100/MO	AGE 65 NEST EGG (WITH INVESTMENT RETURNS)
20	YOU SAVED $54,000	$948,000
30	YOU SAVED $42,000	$357,000
30	YOU SAVED $30,000	$130,000
50	YOU SAVED $18,000	$42,000

Whoa. That is eye-opening. Even for me.

One last tip for talking to parents — encourage them! You never stop being parents, and kids never stop wishing you'd stop being a parent. Rather than telling your son or daughter they are not saving the right way, encourage them to start saving something!

Family Update

Well. It happened. My kids all got into soccer and now I am a "Soccer Dad." It's certainly good exercise, but Dad doesn't have the longest attention span and sometimes he gets crabby by the end of practice.

I find that watching kids' soccer isn't all that exciting. It seems like a big mob of kids just run around, chasing the ball. I never really liked soccer. Why would someone want to play a sport whereby someone could kick a ball as hard as they can into your face? That doesn't sound fun at all.

Ferrying kids back and forth to soccer practice in my minivan is a real reality check. I'm no longer cool. "Cool" is WAY overrated anyway.

The Worst Google Search

I was messing around on Google the other day and typed in: "Baby Boomer Retirement"

These are the search results, in order:

1. Are We in a Baby Boomer Retirement Crisis?

2. One-third of baby boomers had nothing saved for retirement at age 58

3. Tough retirement realities for baby boomers

4. Lack of retirement savings haunts Baby Boomers

5. Baby Boomers Face Reality They Might Never Retire

I'm not even kidding. Those are the first five search results. How could you not worry about retirement when you keep hearing this dismal news?

But are Baby Boomer's prospects really that dire?

Today, the poverty rates among people 65+ is around 10 percent. Fifty years ago, in 1969, it was 20 percent. Nearly twice as much.

Forbes recently published an article titled, The Graying of Wealth. In it, author Neil Howe writes, *"The relative affluence of today's elderly is historically unprecedented. Never before have the 75+ had the highest median household net worth of any age bracket. Today, the typical 80-year-old household has twice the net worth of the typical 50-year-old household."*

Below is the data by which he reached his conclusion.

According to the 2016 Federal Reserve Survey of Consumer Finances, here is the median net worth by age in the U.S.:

Ages 55-64: $212,500
Ages 65-74: $266,400
Ages 75 and older: $254,800

Do you know what this means? The average American sees their financial status improve as they get older. This data is so counter-cultural it is almost hard to believe.

The doom and gloom surrounding Baby Boomers and retirement is profoundly over-hyped.

This kind of one-sided information dramatically skews the perception of most Americans nearing the end of their careers. For at least 50 percent of the population, these articles are completely irrelevant (I am literally getting upset as I type these words).

Even more compelling data:

Forty-eight percent of retirees are able to maintain their standard of living once retired. [17]

One-third of retirees have more money 20 years into retirement than on the day they retired.[18]

I had to dig to find this information. It required me to read government studies and surveys which are rarely cited. But the data is there. It is available for all to see.

---

17. Center for Retirement Research Boston College.
18. Reuters, May 10 2018. "The Myth of Outliving Your Retirement Savings"

If it were up to me, these would be the first five results when searching the term "baby boomer retirement."

1. The Majority of Baby Boomers Will Thrive Once Retired

2. The Bottom 25 percent of Americans Will Struggle Financially in Retirement, But What About the Other 75 percent?

3. The Elderly Are Wealthier Than at Any Other Time in American History

4. The Average Retiree Sees Their Net Worth Increase as They Age

5. Nearly Half of Boomers Will Not Have to Adjust Their Lifestyle Once Retired

Now that is refreshing.

Family Update

Alex, 8, has become the historian in our family. He's currently completely nuts about ancient history (I think it has a lot to do with a fantastic teacher). Many evenings he will expound on characters throughout history.

Did you know that King Richard the 1st was known as "Richard the Lionhearted," and at age 16 he was commanding his own army? Did you know he was married at age 9? Do you know that he was shot in the shoulder with a crossbow bolt that got infected? He died.

Unexpected Retirement Expenses

Unexpected retirement expenses are one of the biggest, baddest boogeymen of financial retirement planning. Settle in, because I'm going to tell you a story about two brave retirees who faced this terrible, retirement ogre.

Joey and Jane Jenkins, ages 65, retired after over 40 years of work and toil. While their Social Security and investment income would more than cover their monthly expenses, they still felt financial anxiety.

"What happens if there is a big expense we weren't considering?" Jane lamented. "You never know what might happen. Who knows? I read a frightening article on the internet explaining how many seniors are hit with unexpected expenses."

Joey agreed. "Well, I guess we should try to live on a strict budget. That way we can save as much as possible… just in case. I guess we won't get to live out some of our dreams in retirement. We will probably have to watch our friends travel, dine, and spoil their grandkids. But it's Spaghetti-Os and Spam for us."

Joey and Jane fears came true, in a sense. They ran into nearly every big "unexpected" expense a retiree could face.

Dental care. Joey never listened to his Mom as a kid and didn't brush and floss every day. At age 74, he needed a root canal and crown, and again at age 82.

While Medicare doesn't cover dental care, there are several options to reduce the cost. If you have an iffy dental history, you should seriously consider supplemental insurance or a discount dental plan. Believe it or not, I would say teeth are just about the largest unexpected expense retirees face.

Major Health Event. At age 83, Jane needed complex surgery to remove some melanomas from her back. The bill they received in the mail totaled nearly $80,000.

Luckily, as long as you receive Medicare and have purchased a supplement, the maximum out of pocket expense in any given year is $6,500. "That was a close one," sighed Jane. "I didn't realize how much Medicare actually covers."

Prescriptions. Jane developed rheumatoid arthritis at age 68. The injections she received each month were extremely expensive. But, considering Jane was enrolled in both Medicare and an appropriate Medicare supplement, she was only liable for a maximum of $5,100 a year out-of-pocket.

There are also a myriad of options lower-income retirees can utilize to receive deeply discounted medications. Surprisingly, in my experience, prescription costs are lower in retirement than most expect.

Car Repairs. Joey and Jane, like most retirees, purchased cars far less often, and put on less miles (after a couple road trips around this beautiful country). Considering the warranties only lasted five years, Joey was upset when his transmission blew at age 78. While the $2,500+ bill wasn't welcomed, it did not upset their financial lives.

Home Repair. The Florida weather took a toll on Joey and Jane's home. During their retired years they needed to replace the air conditioner twice and get a new roof. The air conditioners cost them $4,000 a piece, and the roof set them back almost $15,000. This is one of the most common one-time expenses I see.

Helping Kids and Grandkids. Joey and Jane's third child, Jessica, had a messy divorce, leaving her and their two cherished grandkids in a tough spot. "Joey," pleaded Jane, "We need to help them. Maybe we can set aside $1,000 a month to keep them on their feet. Maybe they can even move in for a while, until things settle."

While not common, in my professional experience, this can be the most expensive "problem" once retired. But it's no reason to skimp and live small now. If it happens, it happens, and you adjust.

Some of you may disagree with my prices, as you may have a bigger roof or really bad teeth. But I'm trying to make a point here. Hopefully as I lay out all the normal "unexpected" expenses, you realize that there are fewer unknowns than you thought. Beyond this list there isn't much else to worry about. I've consulted with many retirees, and these represent the vast majority of expenses. The list is pretty comprehensive.

The solution? I always recommend my clients keep $20,000 to $50,000 in an emergency fund. Keep the money in the bank and maybe utilize a short-term CD or a money market. This will allow you to absorb these kinds of expenses. In addition to your portfolio of stocks and bonds, it makes sense to have a bit of a cushion.

The other option is to finance these expenses as they come, and simply add the payments into your monthly budget. While not ideal, as long as your monthly spending plan has room, you're still in the clear.

Family Update

Christmas has come and gone. The kids favorite present, by far, were remote control cars. I had no idea how incredibly fun those things are! Daddy even went out and bought his own so he could race. I made sure to myself one that's way fancier and faster so it's not entirely fair. :)

Daddy also watched a lot of college football. My kids have a remarkable understanding of the rules. My son will stand up and say, "That's a fumble!" or, "He didn't get a first down!" He's only 9. They also love it when Daddy jumps up and dances.

The Dangers of Downsizing

A lot of Baby Boomers find that the majority of their assets is equity in their home. In conversations with me, they say something to the effect of, "Dave, a big part of our retirement plan is to downsize our house."

Let's think about that idea for a second.

Let's assume:

- You own a single family home in the area.
- You enjoy living there. You've made it your home.
- You decide to downsize in order to fund your retirement and lower your budget.

Ok. So now let's think about your options. Where are you going to move?

- A smaller (possibly a little shabby) single family home
- A townhouse
- A condo
- A manufactured home

That's not to say there aren't situations where downsizing makes sense. There are. Keep reading and we'll get there.

But first, let's assume your house has been your sanctuary for most of your adult life. You love it, but you're considering downsizing to have more money for retirement.

Downsizing for savings is often a daydream, not reality.

For example, let's say you own a $250,000 single-family home with no mortgage.

You decide to move into a townhouse. A decent townhouse will cost you $150,000 at an absolute minimum. Don't forget about the HOA fees. That could be hundreds a month. And don't forget about moving costs, paying the realtor a commission, redecorating or making minor repairs ....

You now own a $150,000 townhouse (which maybe you don't like as much as your last home), paying a few hundred a month in HOA fees. Sure you have $80,000 in the bank (after fees, commissions, closing costs, etc). That $80,000 can produce about $300 a month in dividends and interest. You are almost exactly where you started. Maybe you are saving a couple hundred dollars a month.

Is it really worth it?

Another example: Let's say you own a $300,000 single-family home with a $100,000 mortgage. You are paying $1,300/mo on the mortgage which you've had for well over ten years.

You decide to move into a condo. You sell the house, pocket the $170,000 (after commissions) and find the condo of your dreams.

Actually, that's not entirely true. Barring some kind of real estate miracle, a $170,000 condo is not going to be as nice as the house you just sold.

Now come the HOA fees. Condos are notorious for high fees, which can change at the drop of a hat. Also, don't forget, you may get a letter from the condo board that says: "We decided to replace the roof and we're going to charge you an assessment of $8,000."

But now you have no mortgage! That saves you $1,300 a month in mortgage payments (minus the HOA of $300). So you now live in a condo that you don't like as much as your house which needs thousands of dollars of work and you have an extra $1,000/mo. Is it really worth it?

When does it make sense to downsize?

Here are some examples where it might make sense to downsize.

Your current home is too big. The kids moved out and you are left with a 3,000-square-foot home with a big yard. Downsizing in this situation often makes sense. While you might not save a ton of money, maintenance-free smaller townhomes can be very attractive.

You plan on a major downsizing. Moving from a $400,000 home to a $100,000 manufactured home will create a significant difference in budget and spending needs going forward. Few people like this option.

You have the opportunity to move in with a family member. This can be especially attractive if your child or relative has an apartment attached to their home, or a mother-in-law suite. This is a fantastic way to lower expenses and increase cash in the bank (not to mention bringing your family together).

You have no other retirement assets. This is not ideal, and not the situation for most retirees. But, for those folks facing this reality, selling their home and downsizing to a much smaller space can help them live comfortably throughout their retirement.

So, before you think that downsizing could fix all your retirement worries, really consider the long-term financial ramifications. Do the math. Consider the emotional consequences of moving. And move ahead with caution.

Family Update

My two youngest boys now have their own YouTube channel. They haven't actually made any videos yet, but they are thrilled at the idea.

They want it to be a video game channel where other kids watch my kids play video games. This concept is completely foreign and confusing to me. Why would you want to do this? Wouldn't you rather be playing yourself? Isn't it boring watching someone else play?

Apparently not. Some "gamers" on YouTube have millions and millions of subscribers and huge followings. All these gamers do is sit in a chair, drink Mountain Dew, eat Doritos and play video games— which other people watch. A few make good money from ad revenue. Crazy.

ARE YOU GOING TO RUN AWAY WITH MY MONEY?

It's a tough question to ask, but many of my brave clients have asked it: "Dave, how do we know you are not another Bernie Madoff?"

You've heard a lot of scary news during your lifetimes, and the thought that some financial advisor could abscond with all of your money is terrifying.

So, let's look at how all of this works.

The investment advisory world is HIGHLY regulated, but also somewhat confusing to the consumer.

I am regulated by three separate authorities:

- The SEC (The Securities and Exchange Commission)
- FINRA (Financial Industry Regulatory Authority)
- The Florida Department of Financial Services

As a fiduciary, my activities are primarily supervised by the SEC.

Like I said, confusing. Let's look at this a different way. Let's look at how Bernie Madoff got away with his shenanigans; I think you'll feel better pretty quickly.

When someone signs on with me, we hold the electronic bond and stock certificates at TD Ameritrade. Put another way, I don't have your money. A big bank has your money. If you call TD Ameritrade directly, they can answer any questions you have about your accounts.

As you can see, there are "checks and balances" in place. I do not have direct access to your money. The money is not being held at Kennon Financial. I am not a bank.

The SEC and FINRA closely monitor all activities in my office in Sarasota and of TD Ameritrade. If I were to ever have a lien on my property, or claim bankruptcy, or receive a customer complaint, or even get pulled over for DUI, I have to disclose the information to these governing bodies. They do not mess around. You can check out any advisor's history at FINRA Broker Check (https://brokercheck.finra.org/) and SEC Investment Adviser Public Disclosure (https://adviserinfo.sec.gov/).

So how did Bernie Madoff get away with it?

It wasn't overly complicated, and Bernie wasn't the guy who invented the concept.

Bernie took deposits from his clients and, rather than investing them, deposited them into his own bank account. Simple, right? How could he do that? When you worked with Bernie, you signed over your money to him. There were no checks and balances. The only place to get any information about your money was by calling Bernie:

Client: "How are the investments working out, Bernie?"

Bernie: "Great! Would you like us to send you a current statement?"

Client: "Yes, please!"

And then someone would create a fake statement and send it over. They faked statements for YEARS.

There were no checks and balances. Bernie had all the control. When the crash hit in 2008, clients were asking for their money and the "Bank of Bernie" had run dry. Bernie had spent the money on solid gold toilet seats and penthouse apartments. Then, and only then, did things come to light.

So relax. You are safe. Just never write any checks to "Kennon Financial." I even have to pay people to supervise my own business. It may sound strange, but we need to do everything we can to protect the consumer.

Family Update

My teenage daughter went with a friend down to Sanibel for three days. It's the first time she's been away with a friend like that. I've never seen the girl so happy. She is so social. I remember me being the same way at her age. You're just discovering friendships with people outside the family.

Not Sure What to Wear

Retiring for people whose identity rests in their professional work can be extra challenging. In this week's article, I'm going to discuss practical, actionable tips to help those of us who live to work, instead of work to live.

A woman told me a heartbreaking story once, about the first day of her husband's retirement. He had been an executive at a Fortune 500 company most of his life. When he retired at age 65, she will never forget what he said on the first morning he woke up.

As he rubbed the sleep out of his eyes, swung his legs down onto the floor, looked a little confused and then turned to his wife.

"What am I supposed to wear?" He asked feebly.

His wife thought for a second and said, "Well, I guess dress just like you were going to go play tennis today."

He had no idea what to do with himself. He had neglected to plan for his retirement.

Don't let this happen to you! I have found, especially with men, that retiring can be a very challenging experience. Women seem to be more relational and usually quickly find things to do with their time, such as join clubs, volunteer, babysit grandkids, and help anyone in the family who is in need.

I think about this myself sometimes. I'm a "Type-A" individual. I've been called lots of things: driven, dedicated..obsessed with retirement planning? So am I one of the people out there who lives to work? I'm not sure that I ever plan on retiring. I am blessed to own a business that I intend to run multi-generationally with my children. I fully plan on working until my seventies and eighties.

So, without further ado, here are Dave Kennon's Six Tips to Living an Awesome "Type A" Retirement.

You have to PLAN for retirement (both financially and personally). Don't expect retirement just to "happen." When you go on vacation, you usually put some time into the itinerary, activities, and schedule. Retirement is just a really LOOONG vacation.

Change is challenging. Acknowledge the transition. For the first year or so, you may feel a little out-of-sorts. You may not know what to do with yourself. You may find the change over from working to retired to be stressful. This is normal. You are not strange or unique. This is a big transition. For many people, it takes time to settle into the retirement of their dreams.

Change what you do, not who you are. If you get genuine fulfillment from your work, look into a consulting role once you retire. It is a nice way to slowly and gently transition into retirement. Plus, consulting is usually an awesome job. You are the boss. You work your own hours and usually get paid a reasonable income.

Keep moving! Retirement is NOT sitting by a pool drinking margaritas. The advice I receive from nearly every happy and healthy retiree is this: If you stop moving, you die. Pick up tennis, golf, biking, hiking, bird watching…whatever is interesting to you. Just make sure it involves physical movement.

Volunteer. Or better yet, start a small non-profit for a cause you love. Start an animal shelter. Build homes for the homeless. Start an exotic cacti club. Be proactive. Use your "get er' done" business skills.

Lastly and possibly most importantly: mentor. The happiest and most fulfilled Type-A retirees I know have taken a few younger people under their wing. The best place to start this process is your church. If you are not religious, there are many community centers that are in desperate need of talented retirees to build up the next generation of workers and citizens.

Family Update

Yaya (mother-in-law) had a birthday this week. She is blessed to have three generations of family living in Sarasota. Four children and 12 grandkids. She is basically always babysitting someone.

She was born in Thailand and had nine brothers and sisters. She has a hundred cousins but only knows a few. As a kid, she had no electricity or running water and had to bathe in a river filled with snakes. She has no interest in going back, but she misses her family.

But she will always be Thai. At my wedding she scaled a coconut tree in order to pick a few ripe ones.

IS THE DREAM RETIREMENT
BASED ON A LIE?

What is the dream retirement supposed to look like? This is a question I've often wrestled with over my professional career. I constantly tell retirees to live fearlessly and boldly—refusing to give in to the fear of running out of money.

But, once the fear of outliving your money has been extinguished, what's next? Margaritas by the pool? Golf every day? Dinners out and sleeping in?

It's this, the "what comes next" of retirement, that is the real struggle.

Where did retirement come from?

The concept of retirement itself is a modern, man-made phenomenon. Did you know that our modern understanding of "retirement" was created as recently as 1881 by Otto von Bismarck? According to an article in the San Diego Tribune, "When farming dominated the economy, most men worked as long as their health held out. As they aged, though, they often cut their hours and turned the most physically demanding chores over to sons or hired hands. In 1880, when half of Americans worked on a farm, 78 percent of American men worked past the age of 65."

While I'm glad you don't have to work in the fields until the day you drop, it doesn't change the fact that human beings were not designed to work for forty years and then live a life of leisure for twenty or thirty more years, until they died. Human beings were designed to be fruitful and active as long as their physical health holds out.

Retirement is NOT non-stop leisure.

That is the lie. If you buy into it, as many Americans do every year, you will, in all likelihood, wake up one morning with a sense of unease. A question will nag at the back of your mind. "Is this all there really is?"

Ever since the Industrial Revolution, Americans have heard the same message: Work hard for forty years, even if you hate the work, because when you retire, then you can start to be happy. THEN you can start living your life.

That's depressing. What's even more depressing is the thought that you may work all those years, retire, and find that it isn't everything you dreamed of. Who invented the concept of the dream retirement, anyway? Who has told us that palm trees, warm breezes, leisure, and endless afternoons of golf lead to a fulfilling retired life?

Salespeople.

Investment managers want you to build up your portfolio because they are in the business of selling retirement plans. Even after you've saved more money than you need, they keep selling.

Family vacations and cruises during retirement are fantastic opportunities, but the tourism industry is bloated with offerings designed just to pinch as many of your pennies as it can.

Florida's entire economy is built on the hope that retirees continue to move here!

None of these industries are trying to help you live a satisfying retired life. They are trying to sell you something.

Live that better life right now.

Don't believe the hype. The American Dream of retiring to the beach just isn't all that it's cracked up to be. Your retirement can be whatever you want it to be, as long as it's fulfilling and meaningful to you.

And the best part is, you don't need to wait until you retire to enjoy your life. You can do all of these things right now.

Live a life filled with loved ones, new experiences, and opportunities now, and when you retire you won't be asking, "What do I do now?" Instead, you'll ask, "What haven't I done yet? What ELSE can I do?"

Family Update

We got good news last week! My wife was again screened for any signs of the cancer coming back, and the tests were all clear. She is still recovering from the cancer surgeries and treatments from five years ago. But we feel blessed and relieved. I am so fortunate to have the wife that I do. I don't know how she can raise four awesome kids like she is (all the while supporting her high-maintenance husband as well).

Losing all Your Money

I often hear people say to me, "I lost all my money in the stock market in 2008." Or "I lost all my money in the stock market in 2001."

Really?! Did the stock market go to ZERO?

Never forget: markets temporarily go down and permanently go up. You had all your money back in a few years.

In the 2008 Great Recession, the S&P 500 dropped over 37 percent. Remember, this was a historically bad recession. It took less than four years to recover.

In 2001 the S&P dropped 12 percent, and went down 22 percent more in 2002. It took about 3 years to get all your money back. So, how are these people "losing all their money?"

Most of them aren't, and those that really did lose "everything" are only telling half the story.

What they really should be saying is:

"I got some hot stock tips from my neighbor. I then went ahead and started day-trading those stocks. I was really good at it! Then the stupid economy tanked and my stupid account ended up at zero."

Or they should really be saying:

"I invested $100,000 in a hot, new stock focusing on cryptocurrency, and then the stupid thing crashed and I ended up with nothing."

Or

"I had all of money invested in company stock in my 401(k) and the stupid company went out of business."

People who possess a well-diversified, balanced portfolio are not going to lose all their money. For those who hang in there, it is just not a realistic possibility.

Next time your neighbor or Aunt Jenny tells you about how they lost all their money in the stock market, don't let it infect your own thinking. You don't know the whole story. And not knowing the whole story can be harmful to your financial health!

Family Update

My kids are suddenly NUTS about cars. No matter where we drive, they look at each and every car and call out the name. "That's a Kia! That's a Buick!"

If they see a Mustang or Corvette they absolutely freak. My youngest is constantly asking me questions like, "Would you rather have a blue Toyota Camry or a red Ford pick-up truck? Would you rather have a white Rolls Royce or a green Maserati?"
I'm more of a Honda CRV guy. As long as it gets me there and has good air-conditioning, I'm happy.

Taxes Explained

L et's take a look at what taxes you can expect to pay during your golden years.

Disclosure: I'm not a CPA but I've learned some things through the years. Get ready to learn.

1. State income tax. If you live in Florida, there is no state income tax.

2. Social Security payroll tax. You do not pay into the Social Security system once you stop working. That saves you 6.2 percent.

3. Medicare payroll tax. You do not pay taxes into Medicare once you stop working. That saves you 1.45 percent.

4. Federal income tax. This is the main tax you will be paying once retired. I have more good news! You may be in a lower tax rate than you expect.

5. How about this? Massachusetts luxury tax kicks in when you spend more than $175 on clothes or shoes. It's an additional 6.25 percent above and beyond the sales tax.

6. New York charges an eight-cent tax on bagels.

7. New York charges a 4 percent tax on car purchases in addition to any city or county taxes.

8. California's state income tax is 13.3 percent. This means some people pay a total of 65 percent of their income in taxes.

There is a lot of daunting terminology out there. I'm going to stick with stuff you actually need to know.

1099-MISC: A "1099-MISC" is for work you did as an independent worker or freelancer.

1099-INT: This reports interest income you've received from savings/CD/money market accounts. It also includes any interest you receive from bonds outside a retirement account. This income is taxed at your federal income tax bracket.

1099-DIV: If you are receiving dividends from an account outside a retirement account you must pay taxes. These tax rates can be more favorable.

As an aside, most people believe the long-term capital gains rate to be 15 percent. The truth is that it is dependent on certain factors, which means it often is not 15 percent. If you are married and show less than $80,000 in income, the tax rate for long term capital gains is zero. If you add your Social Security plus your IRA withdrawals plus the capital gains and it totals less than $80,000, no capital gains tax!

1099-R: This is probably the most important form to most of my clients. It reports how much money you distributed from your retirement accounts (IRA, 401(k), etc.). It does not apply to Roth IRAs.

Required Minimum Distributions (RMDs): I get a tremendous number of questions on this subject. The IRS just raised the age at which time you need to start withdrawing money from your retirement accounts (from 70.5 to 72). The amount you need to remove depends on your age. At 72 the amount is around 4 percent. Do you need to worry about RMDs? My clients don't. By taking the 5 percent of their portfolio, they naturally satisfy the RMD.

Stretch IRA: When you pass your retirement accounts on to your heirs there is no need for them to cash in the account right away. This would trigger massive taxation. The IRS now gives them 10 years to spread the tax burden over time.

Standard Deduction: The vast majority of you will utilize the standard deduction. If you are married you can deduct $24,800 from your income. (This might have changed by the time you read this. Check with your local tax professional.) Meaning that if your income is $100,000, you only have to pay taxes on $75,200 after the standard deduction. If you are single the number is $12,400.

The only time you would not use the standard deduction is in situations where you have several other deductions (mortgage interest, charitable giving, etc.). These are called itemized deductions. About 90 percent of the U.S. population just uses the standard deduction.

For example, if your mortgage interest is $15,000 you do not get to deduct it from your taxes, as it is less than the standard deduction.

Progressive Taxation: I find some people can have difficulty with this concept. Below are the current tax rates, as of 2021:

Rate	For Unmarried Individuals	For Married Individuals Filing Jointly	For Heads of Household
10%	Up to $9,950	Up to $19,900	Up to $14,200
12%	$9,951 to $40,525	$19,901 to $81,050	$14,201 to $54,200
22%	$40,526 to $86,375	$81,051 to $172,750	$54,201 to $86,350
24%	$86,376 to $164,925	$172,75 1to $329,850	$86,351 to $164,900
32%	$164,926 to $209,425	$329,851 to $418,850	$164,901 to 209,400
35%	$209,426 to $523,600	$418,851 to $628,300	$209,401 to $523,600
37%	Over $523,000	Over $628,000	Over $523,600

This is where the confusion comes in. Looking at the table above, some people believe if they make one dollar over the 12 percent threshold, they must pay 22 percent income tax on all their income. This is not how this works. Let's say you are single and make $85,526.

The first $9,875 is taxed at 10 percent. From $9,875 to $40,125 you pay 12 percent. From $40,126 to $85,525 you pay 22 percent. So if you are one dollar over, you would only pay 24 percent on that one dollar.

Cost Basis: First look at how much you paid for a stock, bond, or real estate property. Then look at the selling price. You must pay taxes between the cost basis and the selling price. This does not apply to retirement accounts.

Estate Tax: In Florida this only applies to people worth over $11.7 million dollars.

Gift Tax: This is also extremely misunderstood. Unless you are worth millions, you can gift as much as you want. Be generous. You might have to complete a gift tax form for the IRS, but the recipient will most likely not have to pay taxes on it.

In addition, I always talk about how retirees are surprised at how little they pay in taxes once retired. I'm going to include the chart below so that you do a quick estimate of your monthly tax liability based on your monthly income.

Married Monthly Income	Married Monthly Tax	Single Monthly Income	Single Monthly Tax
0-5k	$0	0-3K	$0
5-6k	$150	3-4K	$150
6-7k	$400	4-5k	$350
7-8k	$650	5-6k	$550
8-9k	$850	6-7k	$750
9-10k	$1100	7-8k	$1000
10-11k	$1300	8-9k	$1300
11k+	Talk to Your CPA.	10k+	Talk to Your CPA.

Income is basically derived from Social Security + Pensions + 401(k)/IRA withdrawals. Of course this is not exact, but you get the idea.

Family Update

My oldest son's birthday is coming up this weekend. Grammy is flying down from Pittsburgh and we plan to give him his perfect weekend.

He wants Chick-Fil-A for breakfast.

Chick-Fil-A for lunch.

Hamburger for dinner.

Then a trip to Barnes and Noble to buy books (he is a big reader).

That's it. He's a pretty simple kid.

Do you Still Believe
in America?

With all the craziness in the world, both socially and economically, we need to get some perspective on the long-term viability of our economy and the stock market as a whole.

There are two very different ways to view our economic future.

For those of you who invest in stocks, you're basically saying, "I believe the American (and global) economy will continue to grow and develop as the years go by."

By not investing in stocks you are basically saying, "I believe the economy is going to decline indefinitely."

Let's take these two thoughts to their logical conclusions.

For those of you who believe that we are going to continue to advance as a culture, there are some valid reasons.

- Innovators
- Visionaries
- Science
- Philanthropy
- Technological advancements
- The human spirit

I think we can agree that these reasons make sense. You believe that the economy will continue to grow, and naturally, your standard of living will improve. Remember, we have 200 years of history that prove this exact point. The Dow Jones was 68 in 1900 and it is now over 30,000.

By investing in stocks, you are getting on board with the most brilliant and driven human beings on the planet.

Now, for those of you who say, "I believe the economy is going to decline for many years."

Your rationale may be:

- Unstable geopolitical situations
- War
- The Great Depression Part 2
- Selfishness
- Greed
- Corruption
- Innovation has reached its peak
- We are just waiting for the world to collapse

If you fall into the second category, these reasons can feel like they make sense. Let's take this mindset to its logical end.

If ten years from now the economy has not advanced in any way, with no innovation or societal improvement, it would be the first time in 200 years of American economic history.

But let's say all your fears come true. Wars rage, markets collapse, and we start to decline back into a time that looks akin to the Great Depression: mass unemployment, food lines, homelessness.

Now, at this point, the banks are in trouble, too. Remember, if nobody is able to pay back their debts, banks start failing. If banks start failing, people start to lose their savings. There would be a run on the banks. There would be rioting in the streets as citizens attempt to pull their savings. ATM machines would not work. Banks would lock their doors. Martial law would be declared.

FDIC insurance? It doesn't mean a thing in this scenario. There is no way the government can fulfill its promises.

Would the stock market dive in this scenario? Of course. During the Great Depression, the markets went down 80 percent. The only way the markets could go to zero is if every publicly traded company went bankrupt. If that were to happen our world would truly devolve into anarchy.

What about if you put your money in "guaranteed" products like life insurance or annuities? Same problem. Those promises are only as good as the companies who make them. You would lose everything.

So, in a way, in this doom and gloom scenario, those of you with money in safe investments could lose everything. But those with their money in the stock market might actually walk away with something. It happened during the Great Depression.

So, ironically, those who had their money in "risky" investments, may end up with more than those who had their money tucked away safely in banks.

The next logical step would be that society is wiped out. We return to tribes and gangs fighting for territory. Food, water, shelter, fuel, and weapons would be the most prized possessions. Gold would be worthless. Paper money used as toilet paper.

At that point, does it matter where you had your money?

All of this to make this point: You are investing in the stock market whether you are or not.

What do I mean? If the stock market dives for ten years or more, we are in economic chaos with banks failing and hyperinflation. Either way, you lose money.

If the stock market and economy improve you will get far greater returns than money in the bank.

We are at a point in history where everything is based on the stock market. Either go for the ride and reap the benefits, or only utilize "safe" instruments that become worthless if the markets completely collapse anyway.

So what do you believe? Will America continue to change the world for the better or falter permanently? Own stocks or stay "safe." You need to decide.

Myself. I believe in America. I believe in the power of capitalism and democracy. I believe we will keep growing, keep innovating, and continue to make life better. I believe the stock market will continue to grow as it has for hundreds of years.

I refuse to bet on economic Armageddon. Anyone betting on that has been wrong every time. I'm going to live my life with a sense of opportunity. Not a sense of fear.

Family Update

My mother-in-law is from Thailand. She and my father-in-law live in town and often watch my kids (what a blessing!).

Ya's backyard is filled with huge fruit trees. Mango, lychee, jackfruit, pomelo, durian, and longan just to name a few. If you have never tried a lychee, you are seriously missing out. It takes like a really sweet honeydew.

The most delicious dish is called "mango with sticky rice." The name says it all. It uses a special kind of sweet, sticky rice that has a much different consistency than regular rice.

That, along with the mango and a coconut milk sauce, completes the desert. My kids could live on this stuff. Whenever it is mango season, it's the majority of their diet.

This is a bad Time to Invest

The world seems extra uncertain and crazy right now, doesn't it?

1. Government shutdowns
2. Stock market volatility
3. Incredible political divisiveness
4. Terrorism, both domestic and global
5. A small problem with a pesky virus

This stuff is downright scary.

How could you not be thinking to yourself, "This is a bad time to invest. I had better wait until things cool down."?

I can't blame you for having those thoughts, but allow me to gently plant a seed: This way of thinking could devastate your long-term financial well-being.

So this week I want to give you some perspective. Let's all jump into my handy time machine. We're headed back to early in the 20th century.

(Buzz. Whirr. Beep. Clunk.) We've arrived!

1. The year is 1941. Hitler is marching across Europe. The war is clearly working in his favor. The reality of World War II can be seen on every American's face. News just hit that Pearl Harbor has been bombed by the Japanese. Boys are going to war.

American citizens are very realistically thinking to themselves, "THIS time is different. The stock market could collapse and never recover. Heck, there may not even BE a stock market in a few years. We may all be speaking German."

If you invested $100,000 in 1941, ten years later you'd have $483,014.

Let's jump ahead a few years. Next stop, 1951!

2. The year is 1951. Harry Truman orders the development of the hydrogen bomb. Russian expansionism has become a giant concern. The Korean War begins when North Korean Communist forces invade South Korea.

Why in the heck would you invest your money at this time in history?! A new "red" menace has appeared from the wreckage of WWII. The world is an uncertain and scary place.

If you invested $100,000 in 1951, ten years later it would be worth $446,944.

Buckle up, because our time voyage still has a few more stops.

3. The year is 1962. The Cold War begins to really heat up. The USSR has plans to build missile bases in Cuba capable of launching nuclear warheads. As a side note, the Russians had, the year before, successfully tested a 50-megaton hydrogen bomb.

The American populace is gripped with fear. Schools run nuclear attack drills for students. The possibility of a new World War is staring us in the face.

You would have to be completely nuts to invest your money facing such uncertainty. The possibility of worldwide nuclear Armageddon would get any investor a bit nervous.

If you invested $100,000 in 1962, ten years later it is worth $257,778.

Let's jump ahead to the seventies. Groovy, man.

4. The year is 1974. The Watergate scandal has rocked the country, leading to the resignation of Richard Nixon. The Arab oil embargo, which began the year before, has had a deep effect on the economy. Unemployment reaches historic highs. Cars line up for miles at the gas pumps. The society—economically, politically, and socially—is experiencing some of the worst struggles since the Great Depression.

Investing your hard-earned savings at this point in history is ludicrous. The economy is in shambles with no relief in sight.

If you invested $100,000 in 1974, ten years later you would have $397,874.

You know what? Let's take the expressway past the eighties. Here we go!

5. The year is 1991. Saddam Hussein invades Kuwait. A new Middle-Eastern menace has appeared on the scene. George Bush initiates Operation Desert Storm. Racial tensions explode in Los Angeles following the Rodney King verdict.

What a crazy time to be alive! For the first time, the news stations report on the war in real-time, broadcasting frightening images of bombs exploding and tracers filling the air from anti-aircraft guns. Investing during such upheaval would be nothing short of irresponsible.

If you invested $100,000 in 1991, ten years later its worth would be $337,272.

Two more stops on our way back to present day.

6. The year is 2003. The September 11th attacks have radically changed the way Americans view the world. The USA PATRIOT Act and Department of Homeland Security come into being. Hundreds of thousands of troops are called up. The U.S. invades Iraq. The threat of radical Islamic terrorism seemingly comes from nowhere. Tension fills the hearts and minds of the American public.

Why would anyone invest their savings amid such uncertainty?

If you invested $100,000 in 2003, ten years later it would have grown to $204,207.

Last stop on our Time Travel Express!

7. The year is 2008. The housing market plunges. Banks are hit hard, most of them slashing dividends to near zero. Respected institutions such as Lehman Brothers, Washington Mutual, and Countrywide go bankrupt. The stock market goes into free-fall. The "Great Recession" is upon us.

If you invested $100,000 at the end of 2007 (before the stock market crash), ten years later it is worth $225,863.

I think you get the point. The phrase "This is a bad time to invest my money" can have dramatic consequences. The world will always seem unstable. Don't let it derail your financial independence.

Family Update

The boys went to the barber shop and we specifically told the barber to just clean up the sides. My youngest, Jesse, has possibly the cutest wavy hair on the planet.

They cut it all off. We are heartbroken. They look like they are in the military.

Rental Properties and Leaky Toilets

"Should I buy a rental property to fund my retirement?" This is definitely a "Top 10" question I hear in my practice.

During my 20-year career, I have seen countless clients buy rental properties to fund their retirement. My conclusion? Don't do it. Don't do it. Don't do it.

Now, don't misunderstand. I have some clients, with 20 properties or more, who treat being a landlord as a full-time job. Normally these kinds of property portfolios consist of very low-end housing. They can make significant money.

I'm talking about the retiring couple who buys a rental, usually a few years before retirement. Their rationale? "Once we retire, we can just sit there and let the checks roll in. Not only do we get the rent but we are also building up equity in the house."

I'm going to tell you a story. I've changed the names and a few details, but trust me when I say the story is real enough. Billy and Sally were good, hard-working people who were responsible savers. One day a few years before retirement they watched a TV show. In it, the host showed them how easy it was to create income from properties. "It is a tangible asset," he proclaimed. "You can put your hands on it. It's not like other investments. You own a real piece of real estate which has tremendous cash flow and growth potential."

Billy and Sally were immediately sold. They began to search Zillow. It seemed like there were opportunities everywhere. They didn't want anything fancy. Just a basic home for a renter.

After a month of researching, they made an offer on a house. It sold for $200,000. They used a good portion of their savings for the purchase. They were thrilled they owned the house without a mortgage. Of course, Billy had to cash in some of his 401(k), but it felt worth it. (It's not. Don't do this.)

The home was in a nice, quiet neighborhood. Billy and Sally were proud of their purchase. It was incredibly comforting to know they owned another home, outright. No matter what happened to them financially, they always had this house.

Now, of course, the house was not in perfect shape. It definitely needed new floors. The last owner must have owned big dogs with long nails. They continued on to the rest of their new rental home's to-do list:

- Paint, inside and out
- New, small patio off the back entrance
- Replace the leaky water heater
- New curtains
- Some basic landscaping
- Replace several fixtures

As Billy and Sally were still working their own full-time jobs, these weekend projects took nearly three months to complete. But, finally, it was ready to rent.

When deciding how much to charge for rent they looked at other rentals in the neighborhood. They wanted to be fair so they asked for $1,400 a month (way too low). Amazingly, the first person who saw the house wanted to rent it. What great news!

The tenant was currently renting another place and he had to stay there one more month according to his lease.

Billy and Sally were surprised that the new floors, paint, and patio didn't really mean much to the renter. He was just looking for the right amount of space and at least two bedrooms.

So, here we are, six months in. The house is rented and their dream of endless income was becoming a reality.

Three weeks in, they got a call from the tenant at 10:00 at night. "My toilets don't work," he complained. "I need this fixed ASAP." They had an emergency plumber out right away ($500).

A week after that, the air conditioner stopped working and Sally had to get a repairman out there ($200).

Two months after that, the renter was late on his rent. Billy and Sally felt very uncomfortable threatening the tenant. They certainly didn't want to mess with foreclosure. Luckily, the renter got them the money a week later.

Two months later the property tax bill came in: $3,000. Insurance: $1,000.

Two months later, they learned that the renter had an emergency back home (in New York) and had to leave immediately. Billy and Sally had to start looking for a new renter again.

A few more minor things needed fixing that filled up their weekends. "This is a pain," Billy commented, "We shouldn't have gotten a place all the way across town. Sally's friend, who has a rental, utilizes a property manager."

It seemed so simple and they were tired of dealing with the headaches.

They found a good property manager who requested 10 percent of the rent for his services.

Billy and Sally now really had it made. They didn't even have to worry about the stress.

Let's do some quick math.

Cost from savings: $200,000

Monthly rent: $1,400
   (minus the 6 months to get it filled, so $8,400 total first year)

Upgrade Costs: $10,000

Taxes/Insurance: $4,000

Landscaping *(Billy gave up doing it himself)*: $600 a year

Random maintenance and repair: $2000

Property Manager: $1,680 per year.

Let's look at their year one profit:

$8,400 rent

-$200,000 that could have been making money in his 401(k)
   (-$10,000 conservatively)

-$10,000 upgrades

$4,000 taxes

-$600 landscaping

-$2,000 maintenance

-$1680 property manager

_____

-$18,880 (loss)

Now, that isn't entirely fair. The first year is tough. Let's look at year two.

$16,800 rent *(assuming it's rented the whole time)*

-$10,000 opportunity cost
  (money that could have been invested)

-$4,000 (taxes/insurance)

-$600 landscaping

-$2,000 maintenance

-$1,680 property manager
_____

-$1,480 (loss)

I hope I've made my point by now. Billy and Sally would be lucky to break even.

Of course, there are exceptions. But 90 percent of the people with whom I meet suddenly realize owning a property isn't as easy and lucrative (or fun) as they thought.

I've also found that these landlords never increase their rent. "Ms. Bowers is such a sweet lady. She's been there for 8 years. We hate to raise her rent. She started at $800 a month and we never increased it."

If a property is funding your retirement, it is a business. In business, you have to do what is right for YOU, not just sweet old Ms. Bowers. Even more often, the rental ends up getting occupied by a down-on-their-luck family member or child, who agrees to pay the property tax and insurance (but that's it).

The alternative to all of this? Passively invest your money into a diversified portfolio of stocks and bonds. You'll almost certainly make more money, and you don't have to deal with leaky toilets and lawn maintenance!

Family Update

My 12-year-old son's basketball season is in full swing. I've been to four games so far and these are my observations.

1. There is a kid on the team that is 4 foot 6 inches and another six feet tall. Growth spurts kick in at different times.

2. The best kid has the ball like 90 percent of the time. It's unfair.

3. The talent levels at different schools is vast. The last game was 49-0.

4. Some kids don't look like they don't want to be there. At all.

5. It is a fantastic way for a kid to make friends and have fun (and exercise).

Have you Done
Your Homework?

You need $1,000,000 to retire, right? Not in my experience. Many people are surprised how little money is needed monthly in order to afford a comfortable lifestyle once you retire.

I have done retirement budgeting with hundreds of people, and today I am going to review some of my conclusions.

First, let's take a look at a normal retirement budget.

Here are items (and approximate cost) that I see on almost every budget.

- – Assumptions:
- – Married couple
- – No mortgage
- – Live in a single family home
- – Have one car they are still paying on
- – Go out to eat once a week at a nice restaurant
- – Annual expenses are shown monthly
- – Take a nice vacation each year

Budget Item	Cost
Mortgage	N/A
Property Taxes	$300/mo
Home Insurance	$200/mo
HOA Fees	N/A
Electricity	$250/mo
Water/Sewer/Garbage	$70/mo
Cell Phone	$100/mo
Cable/Internet	$200/mo
Pest Control	$50/mo
Lawn Service	$100/mo
Maintenance/Repair	$200/mo
Car Payment	$500/mo
Gas	$100/mo
Auto Insurance	$150/mo
Groceries	$500/mo
Eating out	$400/mo
Clothing	$100/mo
Beauty/Barber	$150/mo
Vacations	$400/mo
Gifts/Tithes/Charity	$200/mo
Medicare Premium	$134/mo per person ($268)
Medicare Supplement	$300/mo per person
Dental	$50/mo
Miscellaneous	$200/mo
Total	$4900/mo

Surprised? Most people are.

I know some of you are going to fight me on those numbers, but the $4,900 is actually larger than the national average for retirees monthly spending.[19]

Your numbers may be different, more or less, but hopefully you get the idea.

If you don't have a mortgage, almost everyone falls into the category of needing $3,000-$6,000 a month once they retire. And this pays for a nice life! You're not staying at home with the air conditioner set to 80 degrees. You are not eating beans out of a can for dinner. You are leading a full and active retired life.

Of course, your situation may be different. If you still have a mortgage, add that to the total. Maybe you don't have cable. Maybe you spend more money on eating out.

The point I'm trying to make is this: Most Baby Boomers nearing retirement have no budget and no real idea of what their expenses will be once they retire. I hope this gives you a better handle on the numbers.

Remember that it is important to have an emergency fund. Your roof may need replacing, your air conditioner will break down, and dental work can be expensive. These expenses are not included in this budget.

Your homework assignment: Create your retirement budget.

I encourage you to go through the same exercise I just took you through and use your real numbers.

Making a budget for retirement can be incredibly empowering, and for most people, it gives them relief. Relief knowing that maybe you don't need to worry so much about money. And if your budget needs a little trimming, at least you know.

Family Update

So my oldest son, Chris, is 12 and likes to eat. Last night, for the first time, he made a frozen pizza for himself. It did not go well. He ended up with something that resembled a huge, burnt hockey puck.

We ended up getting a pizza from Papa Johns. Chris insisted he get his own medium pizza, while the rest of the family share another one.

As soon as the food arrived, Chris grabbed the whole pizza and an order of onion rings and skipped upstairs to his room. I am not kidding when I say it was the happiest I have ever seen him. I think I have a teenager on my hands.

---

19. 1 Marketwatch, Dec. 1 2018. "Reality Check: Here's What the Average Retiree Spends Every Month"

Everybody Needs it; Nobody Wants it

When I say "life insurance salesman," what image comes to your mind? Probably nothing positive. I spent a short part of my career selling life insurance and it was miserable. Why?

Nobody wants to buy life insurance. The application process is difficult and complicated.

Worse, the very concept of life insurance forces you to think about something most would rather not: your own death. Once you get your life insurance, you never want to see your agent ever again. They are an unwelcome reminder of your mortality. When the agent does come around again, you probably won't see them. Because you are dead.

I have great respect for the sales warriors out there who tirelessly get people to insure their own life. It is a thankless job, but incredibly important. Without getting nudged along, most people will never obtain it, and the consequences could be devastating.

Whenever someone dies, it is deemed inappropriate to ask, "Did he/she have life insurance?" But for many people the answer to this question could change the rest of their lives.

If a mother is at home raising three children, and her husband, who was making $70,000 a year, were to die, she is suddenly in a dire situation. I can't emphasize this enough. She could go from a normal life to a life of poverty.

Actually, let me stop right here for a very important public service announcement: If someone has a child younger than twenty-one, you need life insurance on the life of both parents. Period. End of story. It is remarkably irresponsible to live without this safety net. *If you have grandchildren, call their parents right now and make sure they are protected.*

If you are at home raising children, your death would put a financial strain on the household, as the children would need care going forward. You still need life insurance even if you are not making an income.

How much insurance do you need? If you die, life insurance needs to be able to replace your income. Not just for one year, but for the foreseeable future.

If you are making $50,000 a year, you need to get $1,000,000 of insurance. Why? Remember it's appropriate to withdraw 5 percent from your portfolio of stocks and bonds each year. So if you make $50,000 you need $1,000,000 of insurance. If you pass away, your spouse or beneficiary can (and should!) take the million bucks, invest it, and take a yearly distribution of $50,000. It might seem like a big number, but it's just simple math. We will talk soon about how remarkably inexpensive life insurance can be.

There are basically two kinds of life insurance. The kind that lasts forever and the kind that lasts for a limited term. The "lasts forever" kind is far more expensive. With this kind of insurance, the insurance company knows that, at some point in time, they will have to pay up … unless you live forever.

The far more popular "term insurance" is, in my estimation, the right solution 98 percent of the time. Term insurance is simple.

For example:

$100,000 of 20-Year Term Life Insurance means that if you die during the first 20 years, the company pays $100,000 tax-free. If you live longer, the policy ends.

This kind of insurance is far cheaper because most of the time the insurance company doesn't have to pay anything. The term ends before you die.

To give you an idea of how inexpensive these policies are:

A healthy 25-year-old man can get a $1,000,000 policy for twenty years for $40 per month. (How could young parents not buy these policies?)

A healthy 30-year-old woman can get a $1,000,000 policy for twenty years for $30 per month (it's cheaper because women live longer).

A 50-year-old man can get a $1,000,000 policy for twenty years for $150 monthly. The insurance company starts to get a little nervous that you will die during the twenty-year period.

A 70-year-old man can get a $1,000,000 policy for twenty years for $2,000 per month. Now the company is really afraid that you'll die during the term.

Whenever you buy life insurance, you have to go through an underwriting process. This is where the insurance company checks you over. You will have to turn over medical records, and someone will come out to your house to take blood, urine, and other vital statistics.

These examples above all assume you are in good health. If you have pre-existing conditions the price could double or triple. In fact, many people can't qualify at all. If you've had cancer, a heart attack, or a stroke, you might never be able to get insured.

The bottom line is this: If someone is financially dependent on you, you need life insurance. I know it's not fun to think about. Don't think about your death; think about your beneficiaries and their protection. Don't make this more complicated than it is. Now go out *and get those grandkids protected.*

Family Update

My 8-year-old, Alex, has a truly special bond with his Grandpa. I have never, nor has any of the extended family, ever seen a boy so nuts about his Grandpa. When he's at Grandpa and Ya's house it is like he is living a different life. The kid in is his glory. There might be a 60-year age difference, but they act like two schoolmates. They have similar interests in science and history, and Alex can get all the attention he wants.

DON'T LET THE EVENING NEWS TRICK YOU

I just can't do it anymore. It's depressing, it's discouraging, and it's upsetting. I can't watch the news anymore. While many news sources still offer up reasonably objective reporting, it seems that the vast majority of television news is so painfully doom and gloom that it paints the world as declining into disaster.

It's not just depressing, it's misleading.

If you look past the rhetoric and start examining the facts and data about our world, one could argue that the progress the planet is experiencing right now is the most exciting and encouraging in all of human history.

So here they are. Ten facts about the world that should make you proud to inhabit this planet. (All data comes from Factfulness, by Hans Rosling).

Extreme Poverty

Extreme poverty in the world has been cut in half over the past twenty years. Countries such as China, India, Pakistan, and Vietnam have seen profound improvements in their standard of living. In 1990, 37 percent of the world population lived in extreme poverty (less than $1.90 per person per day). Today that number has been reduced to an amazing 10 percent. According to author Gregg Easterbrook, "The decline of developing-world poverty should be viewed as the focal story of the last quarter-century."

Life Expectancy

In the year 1800, the life expectancy throughout the world was 30 years. This number is a little misleading, because nearly half of people died during childhood which pulled down life expectancy averages. The average life expectancy in the world today? 72.

In 1800, 44 percent of children died before their 5th birthday. (A statistic so grim it's hard to even consider.) Now, the number stands at 4 percent worldwide. I don't know about you, but I can't even imagine living in a world where nearly half of the kids in my neighborhood die from smallpox or polio.

War

The terrible violence of war has also dipped significantly. Worldwide, in the early 1940s 201 people out of every 100,000 died in battle. In the past 30 years, worldwide, battle deaths have dropped precipitously. From 1990-2017 for every 100,000 people on this planet, one person died in battle each year.

Nuclear proliferation has been reduced dramatically as well. In 1986 there were 64,000 nuclear warheads in the world. Today, the number stands at 15,000. While we have a long way to go, the nuclear arms race has clearly been reversed.

Hunger

Hunger worldwide has experienced similar progress. In 1970, 28 percent of the world was undernourished. Today that number has been reduced to 11 percent. That equates to nearly ONE BILLION less people going to bed hungry today versus 50 years ago. While 11 percent is still an unacceptable number, organizations such as the Bill and Melinda Gates Foundation have made it their mission to pour billions of dollars into eradicating world hunger once and for all.

The Environment

While we still have a lot of work to do to protect our environment, we have already made more progress than many people realize. Ozone-depleting substances have been dramatically reduced since 1970. In 1970, 1,663,000 tons of ozone-depleting substances were dispersed into the air. In 2016 that number had dropped to 22,000 tons. That is about 99 percent fewer pollutants going into the air.

Democracy

Democratic nations are now proliferating across the world. In 1816 only 1 percent of the world population lived in a democratic society (all of whom lived in the U.S.A.). That number today is 56 percent. The communist threat is basically over, and free societies are popping up all over the globe.

Literacy

Literacy rates have skyrocketed in the past 200 years. In the year 1800, incredibly, only 10 percent of the world population could read. In 2016, the number had increased to an 86 percent literacy rate. Literacy rates might have the most profound and far-reaching effects on progress in this world.

Clean Water

A lack of clean drinking water has created devastation for centuries. In 1980, only 58 percent of the world population had access to clean drinking water. Now nearly 88 percent of the world receives their water from a clean, protected water source. Diseases such as cholera, typhoid fever, and dysentery have caused misery for thousands of years, and current technologies could erase these terrible illnesses within the near future.

Technology

Lastly, the number of people with cell phones has increased from .0003 percent in 1980 to 65 percent of the world population owning a cell phone today. Why is this such an important advancement? While the overuse of smartphones in the U.S. is well-documented (just hang around with a group of middle school girls), people in developing countries use cell phones to improve commerce and receive life-saving information—and, of course, it lets them see what their friends from high school are doing.

I hope all of this information gives you a good sense of what an incredibly positive trajectory the world is moving on. It is so easy to get caught up in news about petty political squabbles. And it is equally easy to get hyper-focused on tragic events happening across the globe. While this world is certainly not perfect, and tremendous effort is required to solve the problems we still face, we have come a LONG way.

Family Update

My kids are really getting into football. Daddy usually has a game going on in the background on weekends. Of course, when the Steelers play the entire household stops to cheer on the greatest franchise in sports history (you can probably guess I was born in Pittsburgh).

Kids' memories are incredible. My 8-year-old can look at any NFL game and tell me the name of the teams and the cities in which they play. My 10-year-old roots for the Browns because he feels bad for them. My 6-year-old "loooves" the Patriots which of course, is just to egg his Dad on.

How to Escape the "Bad" Nursing Home

T his is the number one most difficult and sensitive subject in the financial advising world. I'm going to try my best.

Will you, or your spouse, end up living in a nursing home? And how do you plan for that expense? I've wrestled with this question for years. And the advice I'm about to impart might sound a little counterintuitive, but stick with me until the end.

I want to be very sensitive to readers who have had loved ones go through this experience, or are going through it now. I offer my prayers and support to those struggling with caring for disabled loved ones.

You may disagree with what I have to say, but after 20 years of planning these are the best answers I have.

So, what do you do if you're retired and nervous about the possibility of having to live in a nursing home, but also want to actually live a little during your retirement?

From where I sit, I see three possible options:

Spend as little money as possible.

Grow your net worth if possible and have the financial resources, if necessary, when the time comes. Of course, this means that for the duration of your retired lives you are going to have to scrape and battle to get by. No vacations. Few visits to the grandkids. And going out to eat consists of early bird specials.

Spend it all without a plan.

Say, "I'm spending all my money. I worked for it, I earned it, I'm going to enjoy it. If I end up in a nursing home I guess I'll have to rely on the government and Medicaid to support me." This might also be a little extreme. You need to find some sort of middle ground. Not to mention, you may wind up 80 years old, healthy, and broke.

Spend a reasonable amount from savings each year.

Start spending a reasonable amount of money from your savings each year. I recommend 5 percent of your total savings per year. If you only spend the money that the money is making, at least you will still have the original principal in your later retirement years; you can use it to pay for that inevitable stay in a nursing home.

But wait … is that nursing home really inevitable?

As I said, I have wrestled with this subject for many years, so let me give you some statistics to inform your decision. All statistics are from Morningstar.com.

Only three percent of senior citizens live in nursing homes. The 2010 US census found that 3.1 percent of seniors were nursing home residents.[20]

Of that 3% Only 12% of all nursing home stays are five years or more .[21]

While not great, those numbers are much lower than most people believe.

Alzheimer's is the number one cause of long-term care needs. Alzheimer's research is advancing at breakneck speeds. Many experts believe that effective treatments could be developed in the next ten years, if not sooner.

Long-term care statistics:

57.5 percent of people will spend less than $25,000 on long-term care.

62 percent of long-term care services are provided through Medicaid. The first 100 days in a nursing home is covered by Medicare following a hospital stay. Nursing homes, including those covered by Medicaid, have improved greatly over the past twenty years.

If you are married and your spouse needs long-term care there are protections in place so that you are not left destitute. The surviving spouse can keep their Social Security, pensions, primary residence and up to $120,900 in assets. There are also simple planning strategies for a spouse to keep almost all the money.

So, how do you plan for the unknown?

From my perspective, needing to be in a nursing home for five years is truly disastrous — both emotionally and financially. I don't want to sugarcoat it. But there is only a single-digit possibility of that happening. Are you really willing to forgo the retirement you have worked toward all these years to protect yourself from a single digit possibility?

What happens if you defer gratification your entire life and don't need long term care (like a majority of you)? Nothing very fulfilling.

Long-term care policies are generally hard to qualify for, quite expensive, and have limited benefits. I do not believe they are a particularly helpful tool at this time. But if you already have a long-term care policy from a number of years ago, keep it. Plans available a few years ago are far superior to ones offered today.

And while I don't want to advocate for you to rely on government programs, I've had several nurses and medical professionals say to me, "I walk around the nursing home ward and the people on Medicaid have the same experience as the ones who are self-paying." I know that's not always the case, but oftentimes the "bad home" isn't so bad after all.

And lastly, there is more support around you than you realize. When my wife got breast cancer two years ago we were shocked and amazed at the outpouring of love and support we received from people we barely even knew. You are not as alone as you may think you are.

The best defense against needing long-term care is taking care of yourself NOW. Exercise daily. Even moderate, low-impact exercise is good for your brain and your body. Keep your brain active with puzzles, games, and new experiences. Schedule your annual wellness check-ups and go to them.

If you spend the rest of your life worried about single digit possibilities you are going to drive yourself crazy. Spend a sustainable and reasonable amount of money from your retirement accounts as soon as you retire. Nothing in life is certain, but living in fear and worrying about the unknown is certainly a crummy way to live your retired life.

Family Update

My daughter now has a good friend, and she can actually walk to her house. How cool is that? When I grew up in my community I always walked to my friend's house. Somehow everything got really spread out nowadays. It seems like you need to drive everywhere.

---

20. Statistics About Seniors. https://www.seniorliving.org/statistics-about-seniors/
21. 100 Must-Know Statistics About Long-Term Care: Pandemic Edition. December 8 2020.

Will Power

J· Howard Marshall II was a billionaire. He passed away in 1995. If you don't remember him, you probably remember his wife at the time of his death, Playboy playmate Anna Nicole Smith. When Marshall died, he left her out of his will completely. The majority of his inheritance was left to his son. Anna Nicole Smith sued, claiming that Marshall had promised her half the estate.

The case went to the US Supreme Court. Twice. It took twenty years to finally resolve the issue. A probate judge in Texas denied the request to sanction Marshall's estate. Anna Nicole Smith did not get $44 million. The will and testament were preserved.

Now, let's talk about YOUR will, and a few other important financial documents.

Note: I am not an attorney. I know just enough to give you the basics.

Is this stuff fun to think about? No. Is it something you've been putting off for years? Probably. Do you know it is important? Yes. When it comes to legal documents you need to prepare for retirement, there are four basic items.

- Your Last Will and Testament.
- Your Health Care Advance Directive
- Your Durable Power of Attorney
- Your Trust documents

Your Last Will and Testament.   All of you know what this means. It basically tells everyone who gets your stuff. For example, you may wish that all of your assets are split between your three kids.

Now, whatever passes through the will has to go through a process called "probate." Probate seems to be a scary word to people, but the concept is very simple. Before the money can be passed on to the beneficiaries, creditors get a chance to collect any unpaid bills.

The executor handles this process. If you have gone through this process, you know that it's not a lot of fun. You should be very proud of yourself for putting up with the hassle. For large estates, this process can last for a year or more. Smaller estates can expect about six months before the assets are distributed. Remember, IRAs, 401(k)s, life insurance, and annuities do not go through probate. They go instantly to the heirs.

Homes, farms, and other real estate properties are notoriously a mess to leave to heirs. Probate is complicated. Kids fight. You need to have specific instructions as to what you want to be done with the house.

Your will may also include instructions on gifts to charities, scholarships or trusts you would like to fund, and even your funeral wishes.

Health Care Advance Directive.   Here's something that is super fun to think about. Who gets to make medical decisions for you if you are unable to do so for yourself? This document better allows your loved ones to advocate on your behalf. It gives them access to all your medical records and allows them to authorize medical procedures.

And of course, this document outlines if and when it is time to pull the plug. (Like I said, not a real fun document.) If you remember the controversial case of Terri Schiavo, you know how important this document can be. Schiavo sustained a cardiac arrest in 1990 that left her in a permanent vegetative state. Her husband and her parents battled in court, and much of the nation battled along with them, until 2005. I don't care which side of the debate you fall on, the fact that it had to happen is heartbreaking. A Health Care Advance Directive can make an incredibly difficult moment just a little bit easier for your family.

Durable Power of Attorney.   A durable power of attorney simply shows who can handle your financial affairs if you are unable to do it for yourself. Often a spouse is put into this position. You would be surprised at how many things a spouse cannot access without a power of attorney in place. Does Mom need money sent from her IRA to her checking account for important expenses if she is not capable? Without this document, you cannot make that transfer.

A common example is selling a parent's primary residence upon their entering into an assisted living facility. You need to have the ability to act as their representative.

This doesn't only apply to elderly parents. It can also apply to a spouse with a sudden injury where he/she is unable to communicate their wishes.

Trusts. I'm sure you've heard the term "Trust Fund Baby." What does that actually mean? Trust documents give you control of your money from beyond the grave. Instead of dumping a pile of money into your kids' (or grandkids') laps all at once, a trust gives you control over how and when they receive the money.

Examples:

"Upon my death, my son gets 25 percent of the money when he turns 25, 25 percent when he turns 30, and the rest when he turns 35."

"Upon my death, my children may receive 5 percent of my trust value per year." (This is a common strategy for charitable trusts. If the money is invested, the portfolio should make an average of 5 percent, so that the trust fund will last forever).

Not only do trusts allow you to control your assets beyond the grave, but they can also protect your money from getting in the hands of people you don't like.

"Upon my death, these trust funds may be paid out to my daughter and her children. In the event of a divorce, my son-in-law has no rights to this money in the trust."

Why is this important? If you dump a lot of money into your child's lap when you die, and your child then gets divorced, their ex could go after half of the assets, including the inheritance. If the money stays in the trust they have no claim against those assets.

What if one child gives all the care to elderly parents? Should they get more of the inheritance? These documents would spell this out and hopefully stop any fighting between the kids.

What if your kids face a lawsuit? Trusts can help protect those assets.

What happens if your child dies, and their spouse gets all the money? Are you ok with that? Would you prefer it go to your grandchild? Or a charity?

I hope this at least gets you thinking about your own death. I'm just kidding. Don't think about that.

It is so easy to ignore these issues. Just do it! Get it out of the way. Do you know who didn't have any of these documents upon his death? Michael Jackson. Can you imagine the mess? Can you imagine people coming out of the woodwork trying to get their "share" of the loot? He died ten years ago and court battles raged over his estate for until just this year.

Family Update

My son has become obsessed with fish tanks. We started with one five gallon. We now have five tanks. I warned my wife this was going to happen. The same thing happened to me as a kid. Buying new fish is so exciting and decorating the tank is a blast. But as soon as the tanks turn green with algae, the fun kind of disappears. It can be traumatic for a kid to see fish die. But it goes with the territory. One of the fish, named Silver Bullet, is very aggressive and we had to put him in solitary confinement in his own tank.

The Name's Bond

I often extol the virtues of the stock market. Yet, I have given very little attention to the bond market. That ends now.

The key to any successful investment strategy is utilizing a disciplined and balanced approach, which includes bonds.

At its core, a bond is simply a loan you are giving to a government entity or a corporation. You are the bank and they are the borrower.

For example, let's say the New Jersey Turnpike needs to fix potholes in the roads. They might raise money to complete the project by selling bonds to the public. For example, they might say, "If you buy one of our bonds, we will pay you 3 percent interest for the next five years."

The portfolios I utilize usually consist of thousands of bonds (using mutual funds, index funds, and exchange traded funds).
It is harder for me to go WAY back in history with the bond markets, because it wasn't closely tracked until the 70s.

The Barclay's U.S. Aggregate Bond Index started in 1975. It currently represents 8,200 bonds with a total value of $15 trillion dollars (43 percent of the total U.S. bond market).

Between 1975 and 2016 the bond index returned an average of 7.68 percent. $100,000 in the bond index starting in 1975 would be worth over $2,000,000 now.

The WORST year the index had during that time period was 1993, where it lost -2.92 percent. The best year was 1981 where it returned 32.62 percent. In the past ten years the returns have been:

YEAR	RETURN
2006	4.34%
2007	6.97%
2008	5.24%
2009	5.93%
2010	6.54%
2011	7.84%
2012	4.22%
2013	-2.02%
2014	5.97%
2015	.55%
2016	5.02%
2017	3.54%
2018	0.01%
2019	8.72%
2020	6.32%

In fact, in the past 40 years, the bond index has gone down a mere 3 times (-2.92 percent in 1993, -.92 percent in 1998 and -2.02 percent in 2012).

Another nice facet of bonds is that, in general, they are not correlated to the stock market. This means that when the stock market goes down, it does not automatically mean bonds go down as well. In 2001 the S&P 500 was down -22 percent and the bond index was up +10.26 percent. In 2008, the S&P was down -37 percent and the bond market was up +5.24 percent.

Bear in mind that bond yields (how much interest they pay) are at historic lows. This is directly tied to low interest rates. Many people feel that bonds will return less in the future because interest rates are so low. There is a lot of truth to this. But if bonds only return HALF of what they have returned over the past 40 years, I still think you would be happy.

So, in conclusion, bonds have a place in a diversified, balanced portfolio. While we may not see the high returns of the past 40 years, bonds are less volatile and a good non-correlated asset to employ.

Family Update

My niece came over to watch the kids for a while yesterday. Her and my daughter decided to make a special desert. They came back from the grocery store with bags full of ingredients.

This was their dessert: It had three layers. The bottom layer was chocolate chip cookie. The middle was a layer of Oreos, and the top layer consisted of brownies. The pan must of weighed five pounds. The recipe was called "Triple Threat" if you would like to make your own.

REVERSE MORTGAGES

When I say "reverse mortgages" to people in my office I get very emotional reactions. They sit across the desk from me, cross their arms and proclaim, "There is no way I would ever do that. It is a scam and I could lose my house!"

Now, to be clear, I am not a reverse mortgage expert. But I have had this article reviewed by a local reverse mortgage broker to ensure the accuracy of the contents.

I will start with the Pros and end with the Cons.

In its purest form, what is a reverse mortgage? It is a loan against the equity of your home which you are not required to pay back until you sell your home.

This could make sense if you consider the other options:
- You have to make payments on a home equity line of credit.
- You have to make payments on a second mortgage.
- If you refinance your home you would have to make payments.
- Who likes making payments anyway?

I'm going to rattle off some common objections people have to reverse mortgages.

The bank is going to steal my house away and I'll have to move in with my kids.

This really isn't true. If you get a reverse mortgage, the only stipulations are:

- You pay your property taxes.
- You pay your homeowner's insurance.
- You pay your HOA fees.
- You keep your house in decent shape.

As long as you do all that, you have nothing to worry about. The bank cannot come in and steal your house away.

I have to pay high-interest rates on the loan.

While reverse mortgages have slightly higher rates, they are still competitive. Right now rates are in the mid 2 percent range for ARM's and in the mid 4 percent range for the fixed rate reverse mortgage product.

Let's say your house is worth $100,000. You get a reverse mortgage and the bank gives you $40,000 at a 5 percent interest rate. Like I mentioned before, you do not need to make payments on the $40,000 loan. (Payments are defined as principal and interest.)

You live in the house another 20 years, at which point the loan (which has been compounding at 5 percent) is now around $200,000. Oh no! What happens now!

Nothing. You can continue to live in the house and when you sell it (or your kids sell it after your passing), you have to pay back the loan.

But what if the outstanding loan is more than the value of my house?! What if my house is worth $150,000 and I owe $200,000 to the bank! I'll be underwater and owe the bank money.

No, you wouldn't. FHA insurance (government insurance) covers any money between the home's value and the value of the loan.

That's right! If you sell your home for $150,000 and you own $200,000 on the reverse mortgage, the bank (and government) covers the $50,000. You never have to pay it back. This is a HUGE benefit.

What happens if my house is worth $200,000 and I owe $100,000 to the bank for the reverse mortgage, and then I sell the house?

You get the $100,000 of equity. All you need to do is pay off the reverse mortgage loan with the bank, and keep the rest, after normal closing costs.

Is the money I get from the reverse mortgage taxed?

No.

Can the bank cancel the loan and ask for all the money back?

No.

What kind of homes qualify?

Basically anything but some condos (but some of them qualify too). Single-family homes, townhouses and villas are fine.

Can I get a reverse mortgage if I still have a mortgage on my home?

Yes, depending on how much equity you have. Let's say you own a $100,000 home and owe $30,000. A reverse mortgage could pay off the loan so you don't need to make any more payments.

How much will the bank give me? How do they determine the payout?

It mostly depends on your age. One spouse must be at least 62 years old.

What choices do I have for a payout?

- You can get monthly payments.
- You can use it as a line of credit and take money from it when you need to.
- You can get a lump sum.
- Or a combination of these if you have enough equity.

The Cons

1. There is a good chance your kids won't get the home.

2. If your health declines and you need to go to a nursing home for twelve consecutive months or more, you must pay back the loan because your house no longer qualifies as a "primary residence." You can always pay back the loan by selling the house.

3. There are quite a few upfront costs. Much like closing on a new mortgage.

Dave, do you recommend reverse mortgages?

It is not my place to recommend this strategy, and I rarely utilize it in the financial planning I do for my clients. But, I do believe it works in some situations. It truly depends on your comfort level and living situation.

Family Update

It's that time of year—the time of Christmas movies. We decided to vote on the official movie that we would watch as a family each year.

- There were several in the running:
- Home Alone
- How the Grinch Stole Christmas
- The Polar Express
- National Lampoon's Christmas Vacation
- A Christmas Story

In the end we decided on a movie which, I think, is pretty obvious: Elf.

If you are yet to see it, run to your nearest Blockbuster now. You may no longer have a Blockbuster by your house, so just push a couple buttons on your remote and rent it online.

Using Artificial Intelligence to Maximize Investment Returns

I was in my car the other day when I heard a commercial on the radio that got my attention:

"Most investors took a huge hit with the Coronavirus crash. That pain suffering and financial loss didn't have to happen, and we'll show you how with a free demo of VantagePoint. Text the word FREE to 411411 to learn how we've applied artificial intelligence to protect your capital so you can navigate and thrive in volatile markets."

You will read my extremely emotional response in a moment, but before that I need to point out: This is a criminal act. They are selling snake oil. They are scamming unsuspecting people.

I heard this on a reputable national station reaching untold numbers of listeners. I've heard it several times since.

I don't know exactly where to begin.

1. If I were to make these kinds of claims I would be stripped of my license. If you are registered with the SEC as a registered investment advisor you can NEVER—never, ever, ever—make claims like this. These yahoos get away with it because of a loophole in the system. They are not selling "investment advice;" they are selling software.

2. When was the huge crash with the Coronavirus exactly? The market was down a month and a half.

3. "The pain and suffering of financing loss." I see this tactic used quite often. These con men feed off of fear. It doesn't matter if their "medicine" makes it much worse. They don't care.

4. The part that completely floors me is where they say "We've applied artificial intelligence." What does that even mean? It certainly sounds exciting and cutting-edge. Maybe they do have some sort of algorithm they could use to help smooth out my portfolio, right?

No, they don't.

Let's think about this logically. If VantagePoint has this fancy software that will help you make all this money, why are they not using it for themselves? If their "artificial intelligence" can predict the movements of the market, wouldn't the developers of this software be unfathomably rich? Why would they offer it to the public? They would be making so much money by "navigating and thriving in volatile markets."

Next, I went to their website. Front and center was:

"Created by world-renowned trading software pioneer Louis B. Mendelsohn, VantagePoint forecasts Stocks, Futures, Forex, and ETFs with a remarkable proven accuracy of up to 87.4 percent. Using artificial intelligence, VantagePoint's patented Neural Network processes predict changes in market trend direction 1-3 days in advance. With this information, traders can confidently get in and out of trades at the optimal time. With nearly four decades and more than $10 million dollars of research and development invested, VantagePoint helps traders preserve their hard-earned capital and create real wealth."

This. Makes. Me. FURIOUS.

Making the claim of 87.4 percent accuracy is ridiculous. Again, I would probably go to jail if I ran around touting these claims. But these guys don't go to jail. They are only selling software.

They use a "patented Neural Network process!" What could that possibly mean? I mean, seriously. It is just a bunch of fancy sounding words strung together.

What is especially sad about these scams are all the unsuspecting investors out there losing all kinds of money day trading using this worthless software. Remember, day trading doesn't work over the long term.

Testimonials from the site:

Jeff S.
"In 2 months I was able to recoup my investment. I have since paid off my mortgage and car."

Sam A.
"I started using VantagePoint 6 months ago and my account has tripled!"

By now you clearly understand that this is a scam. I don't understand how it can be advertised on national radio. I don't even understand how this is legal.

What is the total cost for the VantagePoint Software system? A mere $4,900.

Family Update

My 13-year-old daughter is at a summer camp right now up in Tennessee. It's the first time she has ever been away like this. It's weird.

She was crying when she left on the bus, but the next day she texted us that everything was "awesome." Whew.

How to Keep Your kids Close Forever

I 've harped on beneficiary arrangements in the past, but recently I've seen two more messes, and I want to re-emphasize what you need to watch out for.

For example, Mary opens an IRA containing $500,000 of hard-fought savings. She agonizes about how to invest it correctly. She interviews several financial planners. She works hard on a plan that will allow her to live a secure retirement.

When it comes to naming a beneficiary, it looks something like this:

Advisor: "So who do you want this money to go to when you pass away?"

Mary: "I don't know, I guess my husband first and then split it between the three kids."

That's it. Thousands of hours creating her life savings. Five seconds determining who gets the financial efforts of her entire life.

Let's look at some real stories (obviously names and details are changed).

Story #1

Bill owns a turnip farm in Wisconsin. He worked the farm his entire life. Through acquiring adjacent acreage, he was able to buy up nearly a thousand acres of land in order to increase his turnip empire. While the property was worth nearly a million dollars, Bill would never dream of selling; he made a $50,000 turnip profit each year.

What would happen to the farm if he were to pass? His will dictated that his wife would get the property, and next up were the two sons who would share it 50/50.

Bill passes away. Mom gets the farm. She wasn't really sure what to do, as her husband handled the demanding and complex turnip industry.

Suddenly there is some strife in the family. Son #1 is a responsible parent of two and son #2 loves to spend money. Son #1 wants to keep the farm in the family and collect the profits. Son #2 want it sold immediately for a big payday.

So who is caught in the middle? Their mother. The stress it causes in the family creates rifts that might never be healed. And their mother gets stuck being the judge and jury.

Story #2

A widow dies suddenly from a heart attack. In her later years, she became very close to two specific nieces. With no kids of her own, she began to think that maybe it would be best if they received the bulk of the money. They were almost like the daughters to her. It made her feel warm inside to know that all of her hard work could help make her beloved nieces' lives easier.

Nobody even plans on dying suddenly. At her death, her IRA beneficiary arrangements were examined. The instructions hadn't been changed in fifteen years. Half the money went to a local non-profit that doesn't exist anymore and the other half was split among ten extended family members. Most of whom she hadn't spoken to in years.

Story #3

Mr. and Mrs. Smith named each other as the primary beneficiaries on their retirement accounts. Several years later Mrs. Smith passed away. After a few years, Mr. Smith began dating again and eventually married. Mr. Smith just defaulted to his new wife as beneficiary on his accounts. He just didn't think about it at the time. He was too in love.

Mr. Smith passed away ten years later. The new wife got all of Mrs. Smith's money even with several kids and grandkids in the picture.

Story #4

The parents of two daughters pass away. On their beneficiary documents, 100 percent of the money was to go to daughter #1. Why? Daughter #2 was terrible with money and according to Mom, "She would spend it in less than a year."

Her parent's idea was that Daughter #1 could give Daughter #2 money slowly, over time. This way Daughter #2 wouldn't blow the money.

This is a terrible idea. The reasons are obvious. At Thanksgiving, one daughter threw a turkey leg at the other. Would you like it if your sibling could decide when you can get your inheritance?

As an aside, a trust could easily fix this situation.

It is incredible to me. Someone will spend their entire life working to build up some savings. They care for it, nurture it, and watch it grow. But when it comes to deciding who will get the money, the decision lasts about five seconds.

Family Update

We went to a USF basketball game in Tampa last week with two cousins. (They have seven cousins who all live in the area. How awesome is that?!)

When I went to college at Penn St. I had the job of "sweat wiper." That's the guy who sits under the basket and runs out during time-outs to wipe up sweat. Not a very glamorous job. I did both women and men games. Women sweat much less and they are much nicer to the sweat wipers.

USF had their own sweat wipers and I was sure to critique their techniques to my kids.

DO YOU REALLY HAVE
ALL THE ANSWERS?

D o you think you've learned stuff from my weekly emails? This week I'm going to test your memory and your smarts. Only a few of you will know all the answers (let me know if you get 100 percent). Are you up to the challenge? Good luck.

Note: I tried to put the answers under each question but I don't want you to cheat. So under each question, you will see a string of letters like this: abccdba. The THIRD letter is the correct answer ("c" in this example).

1. What is a mutual fund?
    A. An individual stock.
    B. A vehicle that contains lots of stocks and bonds all in one place.
    C. A way beneficiaries get around the law to change who gets the money.
    D. A stock that you "mutually" agree on with a financial advisor.
        – Answer: babcbdab

2. What is the average return of the stock market over the past 20, 50, and 100 years? (They are all around the same number.)
    A. 10 percent
    B. 6 percent
    C. 4 percent
    D. 2 percent
        – Ebadcba

3. In what year was the last stock market crash?

    A. 2001

    B. 2020

    C. 1762

    D. 2008

      – Ccdbcda

4. Once on Medicare, what is the maximum out-of-pocket cost a person could pay for medical expenses in any given year?

    A. $30,000,000

    B. $10,500

    C. $6,700

    D. There is no limit.

      – Ddcdabca

5. How much money should you save in an "emergency fund" of cash at the bank?

    A. One month's expenses

    B. One year of expenses

    C. Three months of expenses

    D. Six months of expenses

      – Abdcdba

6. The average lifespan of a healthy 65-year-old man is ...

    A. 85

    B. 80

    C. 90

    D. 110

      – Dbadbadba

7. Which investment is the most volatile?

   A. A single bond

   B. A single stock

   C. A bond mutual fund

   D. A stock mutual fund

   – Adbdacdba

8. How do taxes work on Roth IRAs?

   A. You get a tax deduction when you add money and then a tax deduction when you take the money out.

   B. You don't get a tax break upfront and you have to pay taxes when you take the money out.

   C. You don't get a tax break but you can take the money out tax-free.

   D. You get a tax deduction but when you take the money out you have to pay income taxes.

   – AacabdaAacabda

9. How do taxes work on 401(k)s and IRA's?

   A. You get a tax deduction when you add money and then a tax deduction when you take the money out.

   B. You don't get a tax break. You have to pay taxes when you take the money out.

   C. You don't get a tax break but you can take the money out tax-free.

   D. You get a tax deduction upfront but when you take the money out you have to pay income taxes.

   – Ddddecba

10. When are you required to start taking money from your IRA?

    A. 59 ½

    B. 65

    C. 72

    D. 75

      – *Cacdadca*

11. What is the most important variable for your retirement finances?

    A. The amount in your 401(k)

    B. Whether or not you have a mortgage

    C. Have much you have in the bank

    D. Your budget

      – *Dcdadcz*

12. How much money can you take with you when you die?

    A. $1000

    B. $150,000

    C. $350,000

    D. $0

      – *Ddddacbc*

13. If Mr. Smith is getting $2,000 per month from Social Security and Mrs. Smith is getting $1,400 what happens to Mrs. Smith's benefit if Mr. Smith dies?

    A. She starts getting $2,000 per month./mo

    B. She keeps getting $1400 per /month.

    C. She gets to add them and get $3400 per month./mo

    D. She stops getting Social Security altogether.

      – *Adacads*

14. Day trading is a good idea if…

    A.   You have time to pay attention to the markets.

    B.   You have the expertise.

    C.   Never. It's almost always a loser in the long term.

    D.   You have fancy software you bought off the internet for $1,500.

    – Adcdaba

15. If you invested $100,000 in the stock market from 1979 to 1999, what would it have grown to?

    A. $223,500

    B. $150,700

    C. $1,840,000

    D. $940,300

    – Abcdea

16. Does your Social Security ever increase after you take it?

    A.   No.

    B.   Yes. It grows by 8 percent per year.

    C.   Yes. It grows by 2 percent per year.

    D.   Yes. It increases at the rate of inflation.

    – Aadcedjg

17. If you invest in a diversified portfolio of stocks and bonds with at least half of the money in stocks,- what is a reasonable amount of money to take from the account each year?

    A.   5 percent

    B.   2 percent

    C.   8 percent

    D.   3 percent

    – Dbabdacz

18. What percentage of the country dies with more money than when they started retirement?

    A.   10 percent

    B.   20 percent

    C.   30 percent

    D.   50 percent

       – *Cdcbea*

19. On average, how much more or less does a person in their mid-seventies spend than a person in their late fifties?

    A.   40 percent less

    B.   20 percent more

    C.   10 percent less

    D.   30 percent more

       – *Bbabdadlkj*

20. What is my favorite ice cream flavor?

    A.   Vanilla

    B.   Chocolate

    C.   Mint Chocolate Chip

    D.   Cookie Dough

       – *Dbbdbadba*

How did you do? As for myself, I got 100 percent, but I made the quiz.

To sign up for future newsletters

OR

To do your own plan online

(based on my beliefs)

Go to:

www.StopLivingScared.com

or call 941-556-6307

NOTES